Navigating Teacher Education in Complex and Uncertain Times

REINVENTING TEACHER EDUCATION

Series Editors: Marie Brennan, Viv Ellis, Joce Nuttall, Peter Smagorinsky

The series presents robust, critical research studies in the broad field of teacher education, including initial or pre-service preparation, in-service and continuing professional development, from diverse theoretical and methodological perspectives. It takes an innovative approach to research in the field and an underlying commitment to transforming the education of teachers.

Also available in the series

Secondary English Teacher Education in the United States,
Donna L. Pasternak, Samantha Caughlan, Heidi L. Hallman,
Laura Renzi and Leslie S. Rush
The Struggle for Teacher Education, edited by Tom Are Trippestad,
Anja Swennen and Tobias Werler

Navigating Teacher Education in Complex and Uncertain Times

Connecting Communities of Practice in a Borderless World

Carmen I. Mercado

BLOOMSBURY ACADEMIC
LONDON • NEW YORK • OXFORD • NEW DELHI • SYDNEY

BLOOMSBURY ACADEMIC
Bloomsbury Publishing Plc
50 Bedford Square, London, WC1B 3DP, UK
1385 Broadway, New York, NY 10018, USA

BLOOMSBURY, BLOOMSBURY ACADEMIC and the Diana logo
are trademarks of Bloomsbury Publishing Plc

First published in Great Britain 2019
Paperback edition first published 2021

A catalogue record for this book is available from the British Library.

A catalog record for this book is available from the Library of Congress.

ISBN: HB: 978-1-3500-6907-7
PB: 978-1-3501-9878-4
ePDF: 978-1-3500-6908-4
eBook: 978-1-3500-6909-1

Series: Reinventing Teacher Education

Typeset by RefineCatch Limited, Bungay, Suffolk

To find out more about our authors and books visit
www.bloomsbury.com and sign up for our newsletters.

Gracias/Thank You

*To the children who inspired this writing and who will always
be remembered as teachers of teachers.*

*To the hardworking educators who allowed me to learn from their
experiences as classroom teachers.*

*To my parents, Julio and Arcadia Mercado, for their infinite love and support,
and who, through example, taught me to how to live a life in service to others.*

Contents

Series Editors' Foreword

Peter Smagorinsky
The University of Georgia

The Bloomsbury series on Reinventing Teacher Education welcomes this new volume representing the career project of Carmen I. Mercado of the City University of New York. The Bloomsbury series is designed to provide global perspectives on teacher education, illuminating for teacher educators worldwide how they might reimagine their work in a changing social and economic landscape. Mercado's work meets that goal, but does so in surprising and unorthodox ways.

This volume is based on an autoethnographic investigation into the development of a single program in a unique location: New York City, among the most international of international cities. Mercado unveils the historical pathway she took as a native of Puerto Rico who as a child was relocated to New York City by her family due to economic need. She was similar to, but not quite, an immigrant: Puerto Rico is an "unincorporated territory," meaning that the island is controlled by the U.S. government but is separate from the mainland; and Spanish is the principal language. It's not a U.S. state, but it is part of the United States, albeit in limited and limiting ways. Many Puerto Ricans moved to the Northeast coast of the United States, particularly the New York City area, for work in the mid-twentieth century, making them both citizens and strangers, natives and foreigners, belonging yet objects of discrimination. Mercado begins her story as a teacher educator by reviewing the history of this fraught relationship and her family's story within the broader migration pattern of the times, making this volume unusually personal in this book series.

Autoethnography represents a unique form of narrative research, one that relies on personal reflection on experiences to make new sense of the world. It is distinct from memoir in that it relies on more than the story that serves as the object of reflection. More broadly, it relates this experiential account to wider cultural, political, and social issues and events so that the narrative speaks to and illuminates topics of wide-ranging interest beyond one's personal story. The story that Mercado tells in this volume excels in that regard, and the result is a well-woven narrative of her family, the migration movement from Puerto Rico to the U.S. mainland, the impact of this relocation on families, the consequences of this new Spanish-speaking population for the public school system, and ultimately the manner in which she drew on her personal involvement in this exodus and resettlement to help develop a teacher education program in New York that is responsive to the needs of the city's Latinx students and families.

If the Bloomsbury series emphasizes global teacher education, why publish a book that has such a personal motivation and focus, such a seemingly narrow focus on one educator's approach to developing an educational program for one place, albeit in the setting of one of the world's largest concentrations of humanity? The answer lies in the deeply contextual nature of educational work. There is now, and perhaps always has been, a tension among educators between meeting a universal standard of performance, and attending carefully to the needs of the learners in front of them. The goal of Mercado's educational efforts has never been to address a universal standard, as is now imposed upon education faculty by various external assessors. These evaluations are often demanded by people who have little experience with students, even less understanding of teaching and learning, and seemingly no understanding whatsoever of what Berliner (2014a) calls the exogenous, or out-of-school, factors such as poverty and linguistic variation, that produce a poor fit between families and schools for students from outside the White, middle-, and upper-class demographic for which schools have traditionally been organized to serve (Smagorinsky, 2017).

If Mercado's work were directed by universal standards, it would have little revolutionary potential in that it would by necessity be aimed at reinforcing the *status quo*. The *status quo*, however, is the problem for people from outside the mainstream population, establishing one set of norms as standard and viewing everything else as deficient. For a Puerto Rican in New York City, assimilating to these norms requires a surrender of culture that is more debilitating than empowering. Power, instead, comes through the ability to mount critiques that call into question what is normative, consider why it remains so, and ask how alternatives might be developed and put into action.

Rather than acceding to the demands for standardization, Mercado explores deeply the local conditions surrounding schools, including the traditions of schooling that provide invisible structures supporting conventional middle-class, Eurocentric conceptions of teaching and learning; the policy context that enforces those traditions; the customs of the Puerto Rican heritage and how they do and do not provide matches between students and these entrenched notions of schooling; the real demands on migrant students' lives and how they affect their possibilities for both public and postsecondary education; the difficulties of being a person of minoritized demographics in institutions built to support mainstream values and practices; and much more.

If readers are looking for exportable teacher education practices, it's important to keep in mind that Mercado is concerned more with relating her process of understanding than in recommending to all educators the specific, context-bound practices she developed in New York City. She offers a method for inquiring into and addressing the needs of the local population in teacher education. That process involves developing a historical understanding of place-based contexts, including those that comprise the educational institution, those that produce policies, those that constitute the faculty, and those that shape the lives of the students (see Smagorinsky, 2018). This sort of cultural understanding is critical to seeing that teacher education is never a "seamless" process, as claimed by many teacher educators. Rather, teacher education always sits at the intersection of many competing centers of gravity that produce tensions and contradictory conceptions of teaching and learning (Barnes & Smagorinsky, 2016). This awkward fit results in not a smooth and seamless set of relationships and patterns, but a series of overlapping settings that may or may not fit well at the seams or even be constructed from the same material. Simply taking a program from here and depositing it there is not feasible. But taking a process of investigation from one setting and adapting it to another is quite possible, and serves as among the great values of Mercado's autoethnographic inquiry.

The inquiry process must account for more than contexts, however. As a Puerto Rican herself, Mercado has lived the experiences that inform her understanding of what schools need to do to serve migrant students best, and what teacher educators need to do to help teachers prepare for providing a sound, *culturally responsive* (Ladson-Billings, 1994) and *culturally sustaining* (Paris, 2012) curriculum and instruction for their students. If the U.S. professoriate is primarily White, as our teacher education faculties tend to be, and if these faculty lack relevant cultural experiences, then their teaching of pedagogy may promote methods that work against the needs of the students, rather than responding to the needs of students of color and those speaking languages other than English, or helping them sustain the cultures through which they live their lives outside school.

In that sense, Mercado was also implementing what Berchini (2017) calls *culturally challenging* pedagogies for the White teachers and their students, whose cultures are already firmly responded to and sustained by the school institution. Rather than thinking of ways to help sustain the cultures of minoritized students in White institutions, culturally challenging pedagogies are designed to help teachers, regardless of color or ethnicity, to interrogate with students the ways in which the dominant culture has been institutionalized in both tacit and explicit ways. Mercado's approach helps teachers recognize the sorts of invisible structures that she finds make it difficult to even identify, much less resolve, the manner in which school performance is laid on a White middle-class template. This template creates the illusion that those who don't conform to its expectations are not different; they are deficient (cf. Berchini, 2016). Culturally challenging pedagogies help to interrogate school structures to lay bare their ideological and cultural foundations and how those systems advantage and disadvantage students from different demographic categories.

Mercado reveals that she apprenticed with Luis Moll, a fellow Puerto Rican native whose studies of Mexican immigrants in Arizona show how schools are structured in ways that are alien to Latinx people's ways of knowing, relating, and doing (Mercado & Moll, 1997). Schools, for instance, tend to be structured to promote individual competition among students for grades and status. Latinx communities, however, typically work more collectively, developing "funds of knowledge" that are shared rather than hoarded, and that provide the basis for their worldview and means of navigating their environments. White educators insulated from such communities might easily misunderstand collective social practices and consider the students' collaborative approach to be "cheating" and punish it, rather than changing their practices to accommodate the students' cultural ways of functioning. As a Latinx educator herself in largely White institutions, Mercado relates the struggles she experienced not only with students learning to appreciate cultural diversity and learn practices that are culturally responsive, sustaining, and challenging, but with faculty who questioned her relational emphasis over detached analytic cognition.

This attention to relationships also goes against the grain of Eurocentric values on autonomy and detachment, grounded in Enlightenment traditions (see McCagg, 1989). Mercado's autoethnography has a very personal, relational, and emotional quality that is rarely available in educational research. Although I've never been to Puerto Rico, I've spent time in Panama and a good bit in Mexico, and can attest to the availability of a far more expressive emotional life in these Latinx nations and their cultures than is often possible in mainstream U.S. settings. It can take quite a while to exit a room in Guadalajara, Mexico, where I work about a month of each year, because each and every other person must be hugged and often kissed on the cheek before a departure is possible. The city is filled with mural art that is highly expressive and deeply emotional and social. This affective orientation helps to shape interpersonal relationships and social organization, and is central to literacy practices as well. Attention to emotions is infused throughout Mercado's narrative, suggesting that education that is predicated on the idea of "cold cognition" (Roth, 2007) is not only inattentive to the ways in which cognition and emotion are fundamentally related (Vygotsky, 1993). Viewing emotions as adulterating invasions on rationality further discriminates against those students who are more acculturated to emotional expression. This belief in the hyperrationality of cognition is based on the assumption that emotions corrupt thinking rather than drive them, as Haidt (2012) asserts is the case in arguing for the primacy of emotions in reasoning processes.

This emotional quality propels the narrative in this volume in compelling ways. Mercado's compassion for the quality of life of New York City Latinx families comes through in her account of her development of a culturally sensitive set of pedagogies for primary school teacher candidates to employ in their instruction. Her conclusions are not dry, detached, analytic points, but personally important imperatives arrived at through direct experience with the cultural needs of people who feel excluded from participation in mainstream society. Of course, much fine research has been produced in a distant voice, and my intent is not to discard that great body of work. Little of that work makes for a compelling read, however. By foregrounding experience and developing theory at the intersection of what she knows from doing and being, and what she learns (and unlearns) from formal sources such as published scholarship, she works toward the sort of robust concept that Vygotsky ([1934] 1987) argues is only available through the integration of personal, everyday knowledge and formal, academic knowledge. This synthesis is among autoethnography's advantages and provides this volume with unusual heft emerging from her ability to put her life's work in dialogue with other sources to produce a relevant teaching approach for the diverse people of New York City.

To conclude her volume, Mercado revisits course evaluations from her teaching over the years, finding that many of her students adopted her inclusive, respectful perspective and teaching style; and a smaller number had difficulty accepting both her as a professor and her ideas as useful and appropriate. This latter finding is both illuminating and disturbing. Faculty of color in U.S. universities often note that they have trouble establishing credibility with a subset of White students, undoubtedly a problem at any university with a diverse, particularly international, faculty and a predominantly White student body. Mercado's experience of being rejected by some students simply for being Puerto Rican is thus perhaps not surprising.

What this finding does suggest, however, is the need to continue to challenge inequities wherever they might appear in university education. Mercado, as a Spanish-speaking Latinx in a White U.S. institution, is uniquely positioned to see why such attitudes might emerge, much more clearly than they would appear to a person not subjected to such rejection and dismissal. Her career began with her as the only Latinx faculty member at her institutions, included periods of greater faculty diversity, but ultimately concluded with little change in faculty demographics. Without the alternative perspective from a person of color, the discriminatory institutional structures and processes she identifies might not be evident, because they do not stand out in the experiences of White faculty like me and many of my colleagues. We need to be informed of what we cannot see, and we cannot see what is invisible to us. Perspectives such as Mercado's are too rare in the scholarship of teacher education, and need greater attention and influence.

This volume, then, in spite of being a personal story about the author's role in a place-based teacher-education program, has the sort of global implications that the Bloomsbury series on Reinventing Teacher Education was designed to produce. Each reader's setting and demographics will be different. Taking Mercado's approach and transplanting it wholesale to other locations will have limited value. But taking her meticulous, reflective approach to studying her environment and institution to provide local students with an appropriate education is quite possible, and indeed worthy of emulation. For these reasons, we are proud to include this volume as among the first in our series.

Preface

Although much is written about practice in teacher education, we know little about the personal and professional lives of educators who teach teaching. This autoethnographic account gives a rare glimpse into a forty-year trajectory that I have documented through teaching as research. Experiences with many different others have led me to understand the potential of teacher education in a global city that is enriched by a diversity that is found in cities around the world. I find truth in the writings of scholars who argue that we are all influenced in complex ways by our personal biographies (Banks, 1988; Britzman, 2003). How I teach, what I teach, and what I study reflect who I am, a community and civic-minded educator (Edgerton, [1997] 2001) who brings unique experiences to professional practice, and who labors in the interest of vulnerable children. I do so as a transnational migrant who has lived with economic and social inequalities all of my life: in my family, in the schools where I have worked and where I supervise clinical practice, and in communities where hard-working families have welcomed me into their homes, eager to strengthen mutually beneficial relationships between home and school. However, my biography also reflects the influences of historical and structural forces that shape us as we resist or adapt to them. I became an educator during a time of intense international, national, and community activism that led me to find my self in history. These experiences also make visible the need to augment the experiential, intellectual, cultural, and linguistic diversity of educators that children and adults encounter in public school settings, to our mutual benefit (Collins, 2011).

In this book, I draw on a range of experiences to address the question: How do we prepare educators to promote the literacy development of vulnerable children, and push the boundaries of what is possible as an ethical responsibility in a historical, social, institutional, policy context that increasingly imposes standards-based conformity as a response to learner diversity? I share unique experiences as a practitioner-scholar and one of the few bilingual and biliterate professionals in a traditional school of education that serves the nation's largest and most diverse school district where one in four children lives in poverty. The majority of these children are from homes where the dominant language is Spanish (ECS, 2013)—a global language that takes second place to Mandarin

Chinese, by far the largest of the world languages (Romero, *New York Times*, August 27, 2017)—in a nation that has more Spanish-speakers than Spain. I offer a rare look into the challenges and joys of preparing teachers to teach the content area of reading and language arts, or listening, speaking, reading, and writing in childhood education to children who are identified (or stigmatized) as being at risk of school failure the moment they walk through the door (Hamre & Pianta, 2005), and a fundamental basis for achieving social justice (The Social Justice Work Group of Unite). Although I entered the teaching profession at a time when community movements pressed for comprehensible instruction for U.S. citizens from intergenerational homes where languages other than English reside, for over two decades I labored under the influence of powerbrokers who privatize public education and promote instruction in low-level literacy skills in English and accountability through testing as a global, for-profit enterprise (Apple, 2011; Stromquist & Monkman, 2014).

Consequently, I tell this story with the double (or triple) "consciousness" that Du Bois (1903) defines as "the sense of always looking at one's self through the eyes of others." Engaging in teaching as research enabled me to examine my practice through the eyes of different others who came together by chance in formal learning settings. Values, emotions, and ways of relating to others that are fundamental to professional work as an educator have origins in my childhood home, which life experiences and professional work continue to shape. Although I have always lived with the tension of not knowing how others "read" my words and actions, as a pedagogue, in this narrative, I acknowledge these moments, while also making public practices, understandings, and emotions that demonstrate the value of cultural, intellectual, and pedagogical diversity in learning to teach and learning to live in a city and nation that is home to the world (Apple, 2011).

This narrative is also a call to build solidarity and exchange among professionals who "teach teaching," at a time when a global educational reform movement affects teacher education in major industrial nations around the world (Apple, 2011; Hargreaves in Sahlberg, 2015). Although international gatherings of scholars of language and literacy and teacher preparation have a long history (see Goelman, Oberg & Smith, 1984), for full-time, clinical faculty who do the hard work of preparing adults to teach under heavy workloads, these encounters are a rare occurrence. I agree with Michael Apple (2011): it is crucial that we work together to understand and interrupt global and local forces of dominance that are actively working to undermine and destroy public education.

Part One

Beginnings

1

Introduction

Over the past three decades we have lived through changes many times more rapid and of far greater magnitude than those experienced by any previous generation. We live in an interconnected world, characterized by an explosion of information through new learning technologies and the mass migration of people, ideas, and materials within and across national boundaries (Kellner, 2000; Kress, 1996; Pea, 2009). The global migration of families with children, escaping from political turmoil and desperately searching for work, increases an already diverse student population in major cities around the world. This trend is particularly evident in New York City, the only global city in the western hemisphere where children from the major regions of the world attend schools, in the largest and most segregated public school system in the nation (Kucsera & Orfield, March 2014). This diversity is predominantly hemispheric, primarily from the Spanish-speaking Caribbean, Mesoamerica, and South America, and also from Haiti. Asia is the second largest source of diversity in New York City.

Locally, this linguistic, cultural, religious, and experiential diversity also includes American citizens from national origin minority groups originating in North America, Mesoamerica, the Caribbean, and Asia who, together with recent immigrants, forge new transnational communities. Through extended contact and exchange, children who live in homes where Spanish and other languages are central to intergenerational family life develop complex cultural identities and create new forms of communicating in English, Spanish, and other languages. However, this type of contact is less common among children and families who reside in relatively homogeneous ethnic enclaves, as many Asian families do, and also Orthodox Hassidic Jews. Unlike the first immigrant communities in the city, these transnational or diasporic communities maintain productive and emotional ties with their country of origin as they sustain, adapt, or create new cultural practices in multiple locations (Brittain, 2009; Portes & Rumbaut, 2001), with assistance from broadcast and electronic media.

Although this complex diversity also gives rise to a small number of publicly funded dual language programs in English and Spanish, Haitian Creole or Chinese, the majority of children find themselves in classrooms with new and inexperienced teachers recruited, since the turn of the twenty-first century, through alternative, expedited pathways into teaching. The New York City Teaching Fellows Program is by far the largest, and Teach for America the older of the two. Shaped by the influence of the No Child Left Behind (NCLB) law of 2002, both recruit and prepare accomplished adults or elite college graduates with high grade point averages (GPAs) from prestigious universities and majors that correspond to local needs. These recruits commit to teaching in high poverty schools for no fewer than two years, but most do not commit to teaching beyond a few years. Consequently, many are not adequately prepared to understand the diversity they will likely encounter in the classroom, and how it informs the teaching of the core content area of reading and language arts in English. Novices and even experienced educators may need assistance, because "the first essential of a good teaching and learning situation is the teacher's knowledge of children" (The Board of Education of the City of New York, 1967–1968, p. 1).

From my early years as full-time faculty until retirement, I prepared pre- and in-service teachers to address the needs of children from Latinx communities through alternative instructional approaches. My specific focus was on teaching reading and language arts in childhood education, arguably the most important area of the curriculum. This experience exposed me to an international scholarship, predominantly from Canada, New Zealand, the UK, Brazil, and South Africa (in that order). As I discovered, scholars and educators in radically different contexts shared common concerns over how best to address the needs of children from minoritized populations (or ethnic minorities) in locally appropriate ways. Still memorable is Sylvia Ashton-Warner's book *Teacher*, about her approach to teaching five-year-old Maori children in New Zealand, as they made the transition from the language and culture of the home to the language and culture of the school. In course notes from 1989, I wrote: "The method of teaching any subject in a Maori infant room may be seen as a plank in a bridge from one culture to another" or one language to another. Similarly, the "shared book experience" that Don Holdaway (1979, 1982) and colleagues developed as preparation for teaching reading in schools in New Zealand, remains fresh all these years later. The shared book experience eventually transformed into the "Interactive Read Aloud," which is now a core practice in reading and writing instruction through the elementary school years.

Research and practice in the United States has a similar, though now largely forgotten, history dating back to the 1960s, when the federal government assumed an unprecedented role in formulating social policy to address the needs of U.S. citizens who were denied access to an education. Although education in the United States is the responsibility of each of its fifty states, access to instruction in a language a child is able to understand is a right that is protected by the Civil Rights Act of 1964. Locally, these children were predominantly of Puerto Rican origin in classrooms with teachers who were unprepared to teach them, even though some participated in summer institutes held on the island, to learn about children's language and culture.

The Elementary and Secondary Education Act of 1968, the largest of a series of legislative initiatives over a ten-year period, led to experimentation with bilingual and culturally relevant instruction, the preparation of bilingual educators at all levels, curriculum on U.S. communities that are not well represented in our schoolbooks, and qualitative and mixed-methods studies that capture the experience of learning at home and in school by children and families who live in low-income communities. Some studies reveal that all children use legitimate reading and writing behaviors and practices in the informal setting of the home and community, even though these behaviors and practices remain undetected in school (Moll & Diaz, 1980; Moll, Estrada, Diaz & Lopes, 1980). Studies of effective instructional practices acknowledge children's primary language is a resource for learning even when the official language of instruction is English. Instruction also promotes participation in culturally sensitive ways, through positive relational practices, collaborative learning, and informal assessments based on observation and analysis of student work (Diaz, Moll & Mehan, 1986; Tikunoff, 1985).

Other federal initiatives that addressed the needs of poor minoritized communities through teacher preparation include the National Institute for Advanced Study in Teaching Disadvantaged Youth, a Task Force of the National Defense and Education Act (NDEA) of 1965. The Task Force outlined a plan to prepare teachers for all children. In the first chapter of the resulting book, *Teachers for the Real World*, Othaniel Smith (1969) describes attributes of effective teachers of "disadvantaged youth" who live in impoverished communities (a summary appears in Chapter 4). Similarly, The Higher Education Act of 1965 led to the creation of the National Teacher Corps (NTC), a program that recruited graduates of liberal arts colleges and members of minority groups (Travieso, 1975, elaborates on this diversity). After eight weeks of training, interns spent two years engaged simultaneously in university study, work-study in the schools, and work in communities, that included afterschool recreation activities, home visits, and health programs. The nontraditional perspectives of corps members led to curricular innovation in individual instruction and multicultural education. In both name and deed, National Teacher Corps reflected the influence and spirit of the Peace Corps, and some describe it as a social reform movement.

Although comparisons between National Teacher Corps and Teach for America have been made, these programs are philosophically very different. Teach for America (TfA) is a nonprofit organization, founded in 1989 by an undergraduate of Princeton University, Wendy Kopp. In her early twenties, Kopp became TfA's corporate executive officer, and shortly thereafter successfully lobbied for the inclusion of a teacher quality recruitment criteria of the NCLB bill (see Hess in Russo, 2012). Even with critiques of the preparation TfA recruits receive, and lacking solid evidence for the positive impact they were having in high poverty schools, in 2011 the program received a $100,000,000 endowment and the continued support of many wealthy donors. In 2007 TfA provided the template for preparing teachers in the global education reform movement.

The origin of these and other emerging pathways into teaching dates back to the 1980s when the federal government, under a new administration, shifted gears. This new policy context was shaped by an ideology that favored limiting the size of the federal government (also known as neoliberalism), and privatizing public services, including education, a move that resulted in underfunding of public education. These moves were justified by a misleading report issued by the presidential committee on the poor quality of public education, and the preparation of teachers (see comments by Harvey and Berliner in Valerie Strauss, April 2018). A Nation at Risk also recommended that colleges and universities adopt more rigorous and measurable standards, have higher expectations for academic performance, raise their admissions requirements, and engage master teachers in designing teacher preparation programs. In effect, the report was used as a mandate to refocus teacher preparation and instruction that was accessible to English language learners at a time when we were beginning to demonstrate the positive impact of bilingual instruction, an approach we re-invented from existing models to be locally appropriate, as I describe in Chapter 3.

Gradually the structures of support for minoritized communities that emerged from the social movements of the 1960s were methodically dismantled, as the federal government paved the way for the No Child Left Behind (NCLB) Act of 2002 of the Elementary and Secondary Education Act. This was the same law that initially sponsored experimental bilingual and special alternative instructional programs for "Teaching English to Speakers of Other Languages." NCLB introduced "Reading First" (see Chapter 5), a program that emphasized putting "proven methods" of early reading instruction in classrooms in high poverty schools, and allocated funds to states and local educational agencies to implement Reading First instruction and assessment. As a singular approach to learning to read in English, Reading First introduced new challenges to English learners through its emphasis on phonemic awareness and phonics. English learners may not able to hear and distinguish the sounds that comprise individual words due to language differences and/or because ear infections are a common problem in poor communities, a problem that affects children's auditory acuity.

However, coming at a time when investments in public education have been drastically reduced, and its privatization gains momentum, underfunded public schools do what is necessary to access supplementary funds regardless of funding requirements. The multi-billion dollar publishing industry is prepared to respond to the needs of school districts for instructional materials that include costly curriculum packages, textbook collections of stories, and test prep materials keyed to program requirements and to the standardized tests used to track student progress.

This is the reality that I confronted in 2008 after more than two decades as a college-based literacy educator experimenting with different approaches and practices. By this time I had documented that learner diversity needs to be addressed with an equally diverse range of approaches to reading and writing instruction in childhood education. Even with many years of experience, I was challenged to figure out how to navigate the requirements of a changing policy context in the interest of vulnerable children I serve through the teachers I prepare, as a professional responsibility. These complexities give rise to three interrelated themes that I address in this book: (a) Preparing teachers to teach literacy in poor, glocal communities; (b) Connecting communities of practice in the borderless classroom; and (c) Teaching as research.

Theme One: Preparing Teachers to Teach Literacy in Low-Income Transnational Communities

Although definitions of literacy have changed over time and according to place (Luke, 2012), the perspective described in Article I of the 1990 World Declaration on Education for All is one that may assist teachers of childhood education to grasp the bigger picture that is lost when novices and inexperienced teachers are led to focus on the core skills of reading in isolation. Accordingly, literacy is an essential learning tool, not simply a skill, required by human beings to develop their full capacities, to live and work in dignity, to participate fully in their development, to make informed decisions and to continue learning. Wells (1990) explains that although actual acts of reading and writing are individual, the contexts in which such acts occur are inherently social. Thus, "to be fully literate requires the disposition to engage appropriately with texts of different types in order to empower action, feeling and thinking in the context of purposeful social activity" (p. 14).

This imperative is behind the practice that participants in literacy courses that I organize experience during weekly sessions that end with the completion of session logs or written reflections. This encourages participants to share their experiences of the session, and the understandings they constructed from our collective experience. I would argue that this repetitive cycle exemplifies using literacy as a tool to think and to learn from, one that begins in a social activity and that affects us differently as individuals, as Wells theorizes, and that is validated by the range of participant reflections on common experiences. Our primary task as educators is to enable children to experience and to find joy in the power and magic of reading to transport us to real and imaginary places, near and far. In her opening speech at IBBY's 2000 in Colombia, the first IBBY congress held in Latin America, Margaret Meek emphasized the power of children's literature in an interconnected world: When children are more confident in their own national identities, they are also more interested in others ("foreigners, strangers, marginal"). Children's literature has a vital role: it does not simply copy the past but predicts the future and is firmly linked to the social and emotional future of its young readers.

The Interactive Read Aloud is a core reading practice in which learning to read is a social activity with the potential to engage all participants intellectually and emotionally. Much depends upon the book selection and how the teacher brings it to life through multiple, symbolic media, including words, images, intonation, movement, gesture. These experiences are important for all children, but more so for children who have other experiences with print at home and who benefit from a broader range of visual, linguistic, and auditory cues to learn to make sense of the language of books. Organizing reading (and writing) experiences around quality children's picture books that provide English learners with a multi-sensory experience offers the necessary support to construct learners' own understandings of, and what they derive from, these experiences.

However, English learners (or speakers of other languages) are a very heterogeneous group that has become more complex over the years. Addressing the needs of this population includes understanding what Berliner (2014) refers to as "exogenous" or out of school factors that shape learning to read in school, and that result from living in poor and segregated communities. These factors affect family life, health, and access to school-related literacy such as those found in well-stocked and inviting public libraries (see Kozol, 1992, for dramatic contrasts that, through decades of neoliberal economic policies, may now be far more exacerbated than during Kozol's period of investigation). Although all children are exposed to reading and writing at home, "English learners" get penalized for lacking the experiences that middle-class children have at home, much of it centered around exposure to the narrative structure and literary language of quality children's literature long before they enter school (Beck & McKeown, 2001). In effect, these middle-class homes provide children with methods of reading and writing that are discursively more compatible with those in school than the ones available to children from less affluent homes (Heath, 1983; Teale, 1984). Children also enter school with a range of different ways of using oral and written language, and these different ways also shape the literacy experiences children will have access to in school (Heath, 1985; Labov, 1987; Moll & Diaz, 1980; Valdes, 1991). Their language differences compared with textbook norms are likely to be treated as disabilities, further justifying a low level of instruction.

Transdisciplinary scholarship over several decades also documents that children and adults from divergent communities and class backgrounds do not communicate well with each other (McDermott, 1977a, 1977b; Othaniel Smith, 1969; Panofsky, 2003). Classroom ethnographies, in particular, yield compelling images of how social class shapes classroom interaction, findings that have been validated by recent studies of classroom interaction in early education (see Hamre & Pianta, 2005; Pianta, Rimm-Kaufman & Cox, 1999). Not knowing how to make sense of one another shapes the relationships that children develop with teachers, relationships that mediate how children learn to read and use oral and written language, and how their teachers assess them.

It is also the case that when teacher educators and adult learners are from divergent sociocultural and intellectual communities, making sense of one another is equally challenging. Given what we know, preparing new educators to teach the core content of reading and language arts in the world of the twenty-first century, at a time of increased state control over teacher preparation, is no simple undertaking. The teaching of literacy in childhood education has been more heavily politicized, linked to public perceptions of the quality of public schools and to varying political interests (Darling-Hammond & Bransford, 2005). Milner's (2013) study examines the role of teacher education programs in preparing pre- and in-service teachers to teach in high poverty schools, and concludes that they are not preparing teachers to teach in high poverty schools. This is an issue that is a central focus of this book.

As an institutional agent, I believe that teacher education can and must make a difference (Britzman, 2000). I assume the responsibility to address social injustices that result from structural processes (Anyon, 1980; Young, 2005) that create unequal access to a quality curriculum and intellectually challenging learning possibilities based on factors following from class and ethnicity. Heightened consciousness of these disparities shapes a pedagogy that challenges and pushes boundaries of what is "possible, plausible and desirable" (Pickering, 2006). I build on my unique experiences as a transnational migrant, my lived experience as a bilingual professional, and relevant scholarship from diverse countries that informs the organization literacy learning environments for children from indigenous and immigrant low-income communities in a changing policy context (Adamson, Astrand & Darling Hammond, 2016; Luke, 2012). I emphasize the importance of developing teacher–student relationships that are characterized by strong emotional attachments, and a commitment to the wellbeing and development of vulnerable children. New educators need to know how to begin developing authentic, positive relationships with children whose experiences may be very different from their own (see, e.g., Ballenger, 1999).

I also draw on community funds of knowledge in the teaching of literacy that is associated with effective literacy instruction for diverse and marginalized students in high poverty primary/elementary schools, nationally and internationally. Freebody and Luke (1990) developed a framework (not a reading program) for teaching reading/literacy that is adaptable to different circumstances. Referenced as "the four resources model" (see Luke, Woods & Dooley, 2011), the framework outlines a repertoire of practices required to engage in literate societies: coding, semantic, pragmatic/interactional, and critical/text analytical. However, what I find most distinctive about the four resources model or framework is that it legitimizes the integration of students' cultural and community knowledge (what we refer to as "community funds of knowledge") to promote textual comprehension.

Although some teacher educators promote the use of a literacy toolkit that combines different teaching tools and resources, as I have, the "four resources model" recognizes and legitimizes the systematic integration of local knowledge in teaching reading comprehension, not fully captured in the construct of "background knowledge." Evidence from the effectiveness of this approach comes from countries with both similar and distinct forms of diversity, as found in Australia, Canada, and New Zealand, three countries that have adopted this model full-scale (Luke, Woods & Dooley, 2011). However, as Luke, Woods, and Dooley (2011) caution, Reading First is responsible for the resurgence of deficit discourses about children from homes where other languages or "non standard dialects" are spoken. I found evidence for this claim while reviewing the Teach for America (TfA) guide of 2009: *A Balanced Literacy Approach to Teaching Literacy in Under-Resourced Schools*. The guide emphasizes the building blocks of literacy as fundamental skills to reading independently. Even though NCLB has ceased to exist, its legacy lives on through initiatives such as Teach for All, now a global corporate education reform movement that began in the United States and the UK in the 1980s. The movement has been reconceptualizing and restructuring public education across the developmental continuum, and shaping educational policies that have led to the standardization and narrowing of the curriculum in teacher education. However, countries as diverse as Cuba, Norway, and Canada have chosen to invest in strengthening public education, rather than privatize it (see Frank Adamson's summaries on the Stanford University website). Consequently, this is a time when scholars and educators who are committed to equity and excellence for all children through quality public education need to understand and address these challenges from our particular locations, as a global initiative, the second major theme of this book.

Theme Two: Connecting Communities of Practice

Since the late 1980s scholars from different disciplines have been "reconceiving" learning, learners, and educational institutions in terms of social practice (see Lave & Wenger, 1991). Accordingly, learning is social, resulting from participating in activities of daily living, as occurs in the household (an economic unit) or the home (a unit based on kinship) where children are first socialized into the values, beliefs, and practices of their caregivers. Moreover, these communities are to be found everywhere and we all participate in multiple communities of practice on a daily basis. The first two communities of practice that children typically participate in are the home and the school. Each community may be characterized as having a different social purpose and very different ways of relating to others, and is guided by different norms for participating in activities, as the children involved are shaped by different classes and ethnicities. As an educator, I navigate different communities of practice. These include communities of practice that I organize, as exemplified by the literacy courses I am assigned as a college-based educator, and those that invite my participation.

In keeping with this social practice perspective, teaching is conceptualized as a collective process with collaboration and cooperation as crucial features of effective practice (Daniels, 2007). Accordingly, teaching is a multifaceted and complex process, a system that stretches across other people (e.g., pupils, teachers) and tools (e.g., picture books, writing, images, technology), or what Lave and Wenger (1991) refer to as a "community of practice." In other words, communities of practice are collective ways of doing things that bind individuals, groups, and organizations together whilst providing meaning to their actions and aiding learning to both explicit and tacit modes. "Learning" in communities of practice is typically described as a change in participation, but it may be more accurate to acknowledge that learning is social but also individual, as Wells (1990) also recognized. The difference between the two is that when learning is social, it is likely to be observable in the way practices are enacted in a community of practice.

The community of practice that I reference in this book is focused on preparing accomplished adults who are on a fast track to securing provisional teaching credentials needed to become the "teacher of record" (the teacher who is legally responsible for the children assigned to her/him) in a high poverty school. It is a community that I organize and that we sustain through mutual influence. Our shared goal is that of creating opportunities to learn to teach developmental reading through observation, discussions, rehearsals, and reflections on high-utility core literacy practices such as the Interactive Read Aloud, as I illustrate in Chapter 5. In sum, this college-based, clinical practice course allocates time to develop understanding of relevant content, understandings that are reflected in the enactment of core practices as a unit. Thus it is more accurate to say that in this course knowledge and practice are intertwined.

However well intentioned, the course is not typical of college-based methods courses that distill content knowledge needed to teach literacy through lectures or recitation, and also to pass the content specialty exam that the state education department requires. Therein lies the first challenge. The second challenge, as

Britzman (2003) points out in her seminal study on learning to teach, is that adults come to teaching already made. They have been socialized into particular ways of teaching after years of participating in literacy practices favored by their teachers in the schools they attended, what Lortie (1975) refers to as the apprenticeship of observation (see Smagorinsky & Barnes, 2014, for an update of Lortie's conception). The third challenge is that learning to teach is complex and takes time, and that teacher candidates on an expedited timeframe to becoming the "teacher of record" are often underprepared for the first year(s) of teaching in high poverty schools, to the detriment of the children who depend on them to learn to read and write.

Consequently, it takes a lot of effort to transform a clinical practice course that resides in a college-based teacher education program into a clinical practice setting focused on professional practice. No matter the challenge, I consider it a moral obligation in the interest of vulnerable children who are affected by our work as teacher education faculty under our present institutional arrangement. I also agree with Edgerton ([1997] 2001) that when adults give themselves permission to work together rather than working in isolation, "more powerful forms of learning are more likely to take place."

Working in the community is an essential practice in the complex and inter-connected world we live in. We cannot address complex educational problems by working in isolation. As professionals, teachers and teacher educators participate in multiple communities of practice that should assist the complex work we engage in as educators, whether located in college-based teacher education or in public schools. Consequently, preparing adults to teach what is arguably the most important core content area of the curriculum, reading and language arts (or listening, speaking, reading, and writing), demands that we create fluid boundaries that connect different communities of practice, beginning with the most important communities that inform our work as educators. The first of these communities is found in the public school classrooms where adult learners will be eventually placed and where they will organize instruction that assists mostly English Learners to read and write. The second (really the first in order of importance) is the family unit where children are socialized into the values and the social, cultural, and religious beliefs and practices of the legal caregivers.

Over the years, I have participated in multiple communities of practice, locally and nationally, over extended periods of time. Each one of these socialized me to other ways of being a literacy educator and to a range of practices that, at the time, were uncommon in my institutional setting. As co-coordinator of the local Urban Sites Writing Project of the National Writing Project (1991–1993), I witnessed demonstrations of, and came to appreciate, Pat Carini's "Descriptive Review" as a narrative approach to "assessment" that guides teachers to engage in close observations of children, to represent and make visible each child's unique stance on the world, and how they interact with and learn from their social worlds. Similarly, through collaborations with Barbara Flores (1995 to 1996) and members of the Center for the Expansion of Language and Thinking (CELT), I was introduced to miscue analysis, a two-part procedure in which a child reads aloud from a meaningful text, and concludes with a retelling of the story. Analysis examines the child's oral reading in relation to the child's retelling, to understand sources of deviations from the text, without assuming that the child does not understand, a common assumption with children who are English Learners.

However, long-term relationships with other communities of practice are closer to home. The longest of these is the formal and informal collaborations with social scientists at the Center for Puerto Rican Studies of the City University. For me, Centro has been a window on the past, a mirror to the present, and a space of coexistence where we gather to explore and understand a changing landscape of challenges in complex times, which we confront with strength and commitment insisting on shaping a better future through education for Latinx communities in New York City. The historians, economists, sociolinguists, archivists, and writers who form part of this scholarly community have shaped my understanding of the economic forces that influence schooling and the lives of vulnerable children. As someone who prepares new and experienced teachers to teach the core content area of reading and language arts, these scholars have made it clear that preparing teachers to teach in local Latinx communities requires an understanding of the levels of poverty that are found in these communities, their impact but also their sources. As someone who was raised in a working-class home in the 1950s, I admit that I had a limited understanding of the level of poverty that affected children's lives in the 1990s until I engaged in field research with teachers to study language and literacy "funds of knowledge" in these communities, as I describe in Chapter 4.

Similarly, a decade-long relationship with Lincoln Center Institute for Aesthetic Education, organized and sustained by our school of education, opened up my eyes to the multiple symbolic media that shape how we read the world. As I illustrate in Chapter 5, this experience forced me to go beyond language to broaden the range of symbolic media that informs what I teach and how I teach. This expansion includes new ways to contextualize a work of art using multiple media, a very different approach to building background knowledge. Similarly, I learned to use visualizations and performances as alternative ways to demonstrate understandings of a story, as I also describe in Chapter 5.

The third project that remains memorable is a three-year relationship with the largest collaborative team I have been privileged to work with, an unusually diverse community of practice distributed across multiple locations. The "team" included twelve colleagues from the major teacher preparation programs that specialized in bilingual instruction and TESOL in New York City. Although we all knew each other as professional colleagues, when we met to explore our classroom observations it became clear that we had surprisingly different notions of what constitutes good teaching. The team also included exceptional teachers of English learners who sustained patterns of improvement on standardized tests of English Language Arts, by students from diverse language communities; a team led by the director of the citywide Office of English Language Learners, and an action research team from Brown University. Although my role was to coordinate the activities of Higher Education faculty, I admit that I learned the most from the hard-working teacher participants who live with the policy decisions that invisible forces impose on schools. Still memorable are the classroom observations of what teachers described as a "simple interactive read aloud" that so inspired me that I incorporated the practice into my courses even before the literature-based, Balanced Literacy Model was adopted as the citywide approach to reading and writing instruction.

Preparing teachers to teach in local public schools requires the type of collaborative activities I briefly sketch here. If we agree that teaching is a multifaceted and complex process and a system that stretches across other people and things, then collaborative projects between and among schools, schools of education, local homes and communities, the arts and sciences and other communities of practice comprise such a complex process and system. We all benefit from and through our mutual influence in the borderless classroom. The Carnegie Foundation for the improvement of teaching states it best: "Embrace the wisdom of crowds. We can accomplish more together than even the best of us can accomplish alone" (https://www.carnegiefoundation.org/our-ideas/six-core-principles-improvement/). As I will explain in Chapter 7, as teacher educators and scholars we need to extend these communities across national boundaries in the interest of the vulnerable children we serve through the teachers we prepare, as a global project.

Theme Three: Teaching as Research

I engaged in "teaching as research" after being appointed assistant professor in 1988, inspired by a 1986 article by Eleanor Duckworth. As Duckworth explains, when we view teaching as an ongoing quest to understand how learners are constructing their own understandings of the experiences their instructors organize, we are engaged in teaching as research (cf., Smagorinsky, 1995). Through inquiry, a writer explores more than just a topic; the writer produces text, and he or she produces more than the text. The writer produces himself or herself (Van Manen, 1990, p. 126). Typically, course participants completed session logs or reflections during an appropriate time in a 120-minute session, but initially in the last 15 minutes of each session. I read responses almost immediately, and reread them a day or two before our next session, making brief comments on each one. These comments contributed to an ongoing conversation over learning experiences that we shape through mutual influence. In a fairly simple and repetitive activity, we employ the interdependent skills of listening, speaking, reading, and writing that are both content and process of the course, as Wells (1990) describes.

As a faculty, I brought unique experiences and expertise to language and literacy courses as one of two full-time faculty who specialized in the literacy development of children who were exposed to Spanish at home and English in school and through environmental print. Although the topical outline is a legal document that reflects state and institutional requirements, how I enact these requirements is shaped by observations of course participants as they transact with course content and with peers, what their written comments and reflections suggest, and what I have learned from years of teaching and supervising clinical practice in local schools. Sometimes I create handouts with anonymous excerpts as a session review; and sometimes I create a new narrative in the form of a chronology of a fifteen-session semester. It is always impacting to confront the words that our encounters generate, words that capture the many thoughts and emotions that collective experiences evoke. Thus evidence generated by practices associated with teaching as research document how I change as I learn from teaching the same course over the years, even with minor changes to the title. Had I not kept a record of these moments, this narrative of lived experience would not have been possible.

Subsequently, at major milestones in my trajectory, I engaged in a cumulative synthesis and analysis, as occurred when I applied for promotion and tenure in 1993 and for promotion to full professor in 2004. Drawing on evidence that teaching as research generates, I am able to represent myself, and demonstrate that I hold myself accountable for the outcomes of experiences I organize, as a professional responsibility. This self-representation also affirms the power that we each have to represent who we are, and how we are shaped and changed through encounters with others in different social contexts. I would add that this recognition is especially important for those of us who teach against the grain of established practice or who find ourselves in the minority because of our origins, the languages we speak, or the principles and the ideals that guide our work as educators.

Working in a changing policy context during the last three years before retirement, I had the unusual opportunity of assisting the enculturation process of a new cohort of novices entering the teaching profession on a fast track to the classroom, as the only Latinx faculty assigned to teach "developmental reading." Even when the practices that we engaged in formed part of the citywide mandated reading program, we did so in a manner that reflected my distinct way of bringing it to life as someone who was raised in a Puerto Rican household, with many years of experience as a student, as a teacher, and as a teacher-researcher, and who had heightened consciousness that too many Latinx students in public schools are exposed to a pedagogy of poverty, as Martin Haberman (1991) describes. That is what motivated my choice of picture books, how I performed or enacted the Interactive Read Aloud, approached sequential planning, and demonstrated in attentiveness and responsiveness to the needs of the adults I encountered in assigned sections. Through this writing, I have come to new understandings of the significance of this experience for all involved, as well as those who may read about it from different locations, near and far. This last analysis also brings into relief two constants that characterize my practice: (a) an emphasis on instruction that challenges conventional thinking; and (b) reflective writing as a critical tool that makes visible the value of community and collaboration in accomplishing complex tasks and assignments without reducing the complexity of teaching.

Clearly, understanding the complexities of the teaching–learning process goes beyond what is visible, to the invisible forces that shape what we do. As Daniels (2007) suggests, it requires three lenses. One lens zooms out to capture the larger system in which practice is situated; another lens zooms in to examine the relationship between teaching and learning, and a third makes visible social and structural forces that shape relationships of power between/among course participants, when these include members of underrepresented groups who bring nonmainstream perspectives to teaching and teacher preparation (The

Latina Feminist Group, 2001). Combining these three frameworks enables me to understand and explain my practice as a Latinx teacher educator who brings nonmainstream perspectives to a "traditional" practice setting. I make these experiences and understandings public, seeking to reach a global community of practice, for example teacher educators who work in the interest of marginalized communities who share similar experiences and even those who do not.

As this narrative also illustrates, the mission to serve the children of the working poor who reside in transnational or diasporic communities of color is characterized by continuity and change. In the late 1960s, the community-driven Civil Rights education agenda promoted the recruitment and hiring of community-minded educators, and, with it, the freedom to invent and diversify teaching practices and ways to organize instruction. Subsequently, at the dawn of a new century, top-down policies seek to address educational inequalities by improving the quality of instruction through the privatization of public education, the recruitment of "the best and the brightest," curriculum standardization, and accountability through testing. I have employed historical methods to understand the influence of this history on my trajectory and cultural historical activity theory (CHAT) to examine and explain processes and outcomes of my practice, in time and across time. This is the first of seven chapters organized temporally that address three themes: (a) preparing teachers to teach literacy in low-income, transnational communities; (b) connecting communities of practice; and (c) teaching as research. The three themes are intersected by the theme of continuity and change in educator preparation. The remaining six chapters are summarized next.

Part 1: A Teacher Educator's Autobiography

Chapter 2: Becoming an Educator

This chapter is autobiographical, informed by recent theorizing on influences that shape the trajectories of our lives. In my case, early experiences at home and in school established the foundation for the educator I became. Although change is constant, my stance as an educator began to take shape through experiences in family life and in school. The chapter also examines differences between immigrants and "national origin minority children," American children who live in homes and communities where languages other than English are spoken, as I did.

Part 2: Learning to Teach

Chapter 3: Learning to Teach Children

I did not plan on becoming a teacher; the teaching profession found me, opening the door to a new, experimental elementary school for children from Spanish-speaking homes. At this small school, in a low-income community, I was socialized into teaching by a dedicated professional group of educators, Latinx in majority, and children who made coming to school joyful.

Chapter 4: Becoming a Teaching Educator

After seven years, uncommon experiences teaching the school curriculum in English and Spanish led to an invitation to join a new bilingual teacher preparation program in the city university system, as the new field of Bilingual "Teacher Training" (now professional development) was in its infancy. This is where I learned to teach adults as an adjunct instructor in the new bilingual teacher preparation programs in childhood education.

Part 3: Teaching to Learn in the Community

Chapter 5: Teaching to Learn in a Changing Policy Context

This chapter describes challenges I confront in preparing accomplished adults to teach "developmental reading" in high needs schools, in a first semester, college-based course, organized as a community of practice. Emphasis is on the practices and materials that emerge from collaborations with other communities of practice, that I adapt and use to demonstrate how to organize challenging and engaging literacy learning environment in the primary (grades one to three) and elementary grades (grades four to six). This unusual (and intimidating) approach in college-based teacher preparation creates unanticipated benefits and opportunities to learn to teach in a first semester course.

Chapter 6: Teaching as Learning in Practice

I reengage with evidence generated through reflective writing that captures in-the-moment experiences, over time, guided by new theoretical lenses that yield a more nuanced and situated view of collective activity. A retrospective-prospective analysis makes visible themes of continuity and change over a forty-year professional trajectory, where collaborative practice and reflective writing and dialogue are constants, as are efforts to build and sustain relationships of trust with and among strangers who come together by chance each semester. These experiences yield new understandings of the knowledge–practice connection as integral rather than distinct aspects of learning to teach.

Chapter 7: On Reimagining Educator Preparation

The past serves as a guide to begin to reimagine educator preparation and to work for change from our locations as community-minded educators, drawing on lessons learned in acting against educational inequalities through collaborations with other communities of practice, within and across national boundaries.

Becoming an Educator

As I discovered through the act of writing, the origins of the educator I became may be found in family life and the first years of schooling, two years after we left Puerto Rico, the Caribbean island that was home, to start a new life in New York. My parents traveled north in search of a livable income that was not to be found on the island they loved, and that they would not have left had this not been the case.

Although we settled in New York City, we arrived as migrants who spoke Spanish and who were also American citizens because the island that is my birthplace is neither a foreign country nor a U.S. state. Puerto Rico has sustained a relationship with the Spanish language from 400 years of Spanish colonization; and since 1898 with English, as an unincorporated territory conceded to the United States by Spain to bring an end to the Spanish–American War. The part that is difficult for many to grasp is that Puerto Ricans became U.S. citizens as Spanish-speakers through an act of Congress in 1917. For most born on the island, English is our second language. However, ours is also a second-class citizenship because Puerto Ricans who reside on the island cannot vote in U.S. elections, and have no Congressional representation. In commerce, trade with countries other than the United States is prohibited.

Even though Spanish and English are official languages, Spanish remains the language of family life wherever Puerto Ricans reside, with some generational differences. Still, Puerto Ricans are considered to be the most bilingual people in a hemisphere where both languages are equally important, and in a global city, New York, that is now to the largest and most diverse of the U.S. Latinx communities. Although the right to a public education stateside should make instruction accessible in Spanish and English for Puerto Ricans who speak little or no English, it is not; nor do educators understand that even those of us who are fluent in English reveal the influence of Spanish in speaking and writing in English. Spanish and English are integral to who we are. Some scholars claim that these two languages are now so tightly intertwined that they constitute one language (Urciuoli, 1996), explaining why Spanish is in my English and English is in my Spanish, in complex and not so transparent ways.

Some social scientists explain that Puerto Ricans were pushed out of the island beginning in the depression years, to alleviate the impact of U.S. economic policies on the island, including a shift from an agrarian to a manufacturing economy. My father's unpublished memoir chronicles his struggle (and anguish) at not being able to earn a livable wage to support a growing family, neither in Dorado nor in San Juan. Encouraged by his older brother, he ventured north alone in 1947, to apply for job openings at Silvercup, a large commercial bakery at the foot of the Queensboro Bridge in New York City. While in the city, Dad became acquainted with East Harlem/El Barrio, where my aunt lives with hometown friends. The neighborhood known as Italian Harlem was transformed with the arrival of large numbers of islanders to the city into Spanish-speaking El Barrio, which, until recently, was the largest of the Puerto Rican enclaves in New York City, and in the United States.

On April 23, 1948, at a time when most Puerto Ricans found it difficult to find stable, well-paid jobs in New York, Dad was fortunate to find a union job at Silvercup, which served as his primary source of income for close to 30 years, until an on-the-job injury led to his retirement in 1970. In July of 1948, Dad returned for his young family, lacking the money needed to pay for four one-way tickets to New York and bus transportation to Manhattan. I estimate travel costs at several hundred dollars, considering that the airfare was about fifty dollars per person. Mom's oldest sister helped Dad sell the few pieces of furniture we owned, and with airfare and bus transportation money in their pockets, my parents left the small-town life they led on the island for a new life in what was, at the time, the largest, densest, and most diverse urban center in the nation.

We made history as part of the first large airborne migration of Puerto Ricans to New York City, ending an era in which islanders journeyed north by more costly and lengthier steamship travel. I consider it significant that my parents were mature, responsible adults in their early thirties, with an eighth grade education (at the time, the equivalent of a high school education), and a knowledge of English, a required school subject. However, challenges confronted us the moment we arrived. In his memoir Dad details how he almost got into a fight with the driver of the bus to Manhattan for complaining that there were no empty seats left. The driver gave dad an ultimatum: either get on the bus or walk. My parents remained standing after many hours of travel on the long ride to Manhattan, my mother cradling me in her arms, and dad my older brother. I was exhausted reading about their odyssey, undaunted as they confronted the first of many challenges life would present, as we began a new life in a top floor, two-bedroom apartment in an old tenement building near the East River, which we shared with my aunt and mom's sister-in-law.

As the seasons changed, being close to the river in a building with inadequate heating on cold winter nights, Dad risked lighting the stove to keep us warm. During the day, we dressed appropriately, but never warmly enough, as I realized from studying old photographs mailed along with long missives to island family. Gradually, we adapted to another island, New York City, where days were often dark during harsh winters, keeping us indoors most of the time. We celebrated the arrival of warmer weather by taking walks in Jefferson Park dressed in our finest attire. The challenges we faced were miniscule in comparison with those faced by people who came in search of employment and encountered discrimination and racially motivated violence, as Sánchez Korrol (1983) describes. My paternal grandfather was among those who encountered abuse, which he detailed in a 1954 letter to his eldest daughter Eugenia, who was recruited for low-wage migrant work in Haverstraw, New York. Although New York City had its shares of abuses, it had more sources of support.

What I find most interesting as a literacy educator is a literary tradition that began in Cuba in 1862, when tobacco workers paid readers (*lectores*) to read aloud news reports and literary works of interest as they engaged in the tedious work of cutting and rolling tobacco leaves (Mangual, 1996). The tradition migrated (because ideas and cultural practices migrate along with people and work) to Puerto Rico, the Dominican Republic, and Mexico before entering the United States through Florida in Tampa and Key West, and eventually heading north to New York City. Alternating listening to animated readings with occasional lively discussions, tobacco workers with little formal schooling were transformed into the most enlightened members of the working class. A century or so later, in 1999, I discovered the "Interactive Read Aloud" practice in a New York City elementary school, as I describe in Chapter 5.

In addition to tobacco workers, some of the leading intellectuals and writers who actively worked for emancipation from Spanish colonialism found safe haven to gather and plan their moves in a city that writers and intellectuals from the Americas found welcoming. Leading thinkers and writers from the Caribbean, shaped by new and established intellectual traditions from Europe and the Americas—Eugenio Maria de Hostos and Emeterio Betances from Puerto Rico, and Jose Marti from Cuba—also engaged in intellectual exchanges with local tobacco workers. Hostos, one of the most influential educational theorists and practitioners from the Americas, thought deeply about the role of education in preparing the people of Puerto Rico for freedom in the democratic society he and other patriots envisioned. To advance that goal, he developed a curriculum and pedagogical approach that fostered inquiry and critical thinking, ideas that began to take shape and develop through encounters with European intellectuals, and those from the Spanish-speaking Americas.

Because Hostos's ideas posed a threat to educational programs organized by the Catholic Church, he conceived of the Normal School, or teacher's college, as an independent entity that would prepare educators dedicated to the formation of a citizenry with the capacity to reason and to exercise sound judgment. The teacher preparation program where I spent most of my professional life started out as a normal school for young women, and eventually transformed into a large liberal arts college. Although Hostos succeeded in making this vision a reality in the newly independent nations of the Dominican Republic and Chile, he chose to be buried in the Dominican Republic, where he is revered as national hero, until Puerto Rico becomes an independent nation, at which point his wish is to be reinterred in his island home. Marti is similarly a prolific thinker, writer, educator, and activist, who published the first magazine for children in Spanish (*La Edad de Oro*/The Golden Age) from Brooklyn, where he also wrote columns in major English and Spanish newspapers. My parents found traces of this history in East Harlem, which now inspires thinking about the future.

The challenges that my parents confronted in those early years involved learning to navigate and adjust to life in a large, urban center, so very different from the small town life they knew, where neighbors were like family. Given the fast pace of change in overcrowded immigrant communities, newcomers were typically the targets of discrimination by those who had come before, even though we lived in an area where Puerto Ricans had settled from the late 1920s (Sánchez Korrol, 1983). My parents had a strong network of support, from family to hometown friends and new acquaintances they could turn to for support, as a mature, married couple. Through first encounters with different "others," we gained consciousness of language and cultural differences as well as our common migration story: that we all came to this country (or this geographical region), not always voluntarily, but always in search of a better life, and grateful for the opportunities it offered, as Dad liked to say. Adapting to our new home meant co-existing peacefully with neighbors whose language and cultural practices were different from our own, but where English was our common language.

In 1949, our second year in El Barrio, Dad found a larger apartment on East 114th St. near a major public transportation center, to accommodate the arrival of my twin brother and sister. Luckily, by now, both parents had steady employment and their salaries combined yielded a livable wage, supplemented by contributions from my aunts and uncle and high-interest loans from Household Finance. My Aunt Betsy (short for Basilisa) came up from Puerto Rico to serve as a sponsor for Uncle Eugene when he was released from prison following his arrest at a local Italian bar shortly after his arrival. At the bar, during an escalation of tensions, someone had placed a loaded gun in his coat pocket, an injustice that affected his life and motivated my grandmother to make a rare trip to New York to check in on her "children," all living beneath one roof.

During the next two years, our apartment was transformed into a hometown (social) club on weekends, where friends and family from Dorado gathered for companionship, advice, and great home cooking. I have dreamlike memories of kitchen aromas, the sounds of lively conversation, music, and laughter as we celebrated birthdays, christenings, and other special occasions until the wee hours of the morning. Photographs shared with family in Puerto Rico document these special occasions: one of Dad smiling as he led the conga line using a large pot for cooking rice as a drum. While most activities were intergenerational, some were not for children. Mom was a respected spiritual "healer," and soon after arrival formed part of a community of healers that gathered regularly to help others deal with life's challenges and hardships. Mom did not hesitate to leave us under their care on days when the islander she hired to cook and care for us was unable to come.

Dad became familiar with local institutional (and political) sources of support, and knew where to go for help. He spoke fondly of Vito Marcantonio, the Italian-American Congressman representing East Harlem, an unusual, community-oriented politician who attended to the needs of the poor, and who enjoyed the support of the three largest communities in his district: African American, Puerto Rican, and Italian. In the library and archives of the Puerto Rican diaspora at Hunter College, I discovered that Marcantonio had been a student of Leonard Covello, an Italian-American educator whom I had come to know as the community-oriented principal of Benjamin Franklin High School (1934 to 1954). Covello is memorable because he addressed the high dropout rate of Italian and Puerto Rican youth (mostly males), by enacting a different vision of schooling, and a curriculum that builds on students' lives outside school, what we now refer to as "community funds of knowledge" (see Gonzalez, Moll & Amanti, 2005). Both Covello and Marcantonio had close ties with the Puerto Rican community of East Harlem, respected as community leaders who worked tirelessly in defense of all vulnerable migrants and immigrants.

First School Experiences

My destiny as an educator began to take shape during my first years in East Harlem. Two years after we arrived, my parents made the decision to enroll me in a parochial school, expecting that it would provide the support I needed as a child who was new to English. I assume they knew that the school hired a new principal who had lived in Puerto Rico and was fluent in Spanish, at a time when there were few classroom teachers who spoke Spanish, and thousands of new Puerto Rican students had enrolled in local public schools. Commander Shea Memorial School, the unusual Catholic School named after a heroic naval officer and not a saint, was originally built in 1909 as a large Talmud Torah or weekday supplementary school with capacity for 2,000, where children of community-conscious Jewish immigrants studied their cultural heritage, language, and religious beliefs for a small contribution. I found these details interesting as an adult, because in the 1950s the Puerto Rican community was aggressively advocating for bilingual instruction in public schools given the high dropout rate among recent arrivals. Noticing commonalities and differences between these two communities allowed me an understanding of our struggles for public, bilingual education more clearly, as well as the injustices of a system unable or unwilling to comprehend our right to public education in a language we could understand. Seeing the potential of this large building to accommodate a growing number of Puerto Rican children being raised as Catholics, the Archdioceses of New York purchased the building and transformed it into a school intended to serve the needs of the growing Puerto Rican community. In 1943, Commander Shea opened its doors. I walked in seven years later, and walked out a year after that, transferring to my local public elementary school for second grade because of a traumatizing incident in my first weeks at the school.

Although I was used to playing on the fire escape outside the window of our top floor apartment, I found the fire escape at Commander Shea larger and more intimidating. I climbed it, evoking fears that were apparent to peers who tugged at my skirt as we made our way up to our classrooms. At an assembly in the courtyard one morning, the Mother Superior called me to her, raised the large bell that she used to call us to order, and struck me on my head as others stared in silence. As an educator, I am outraged that a young child who is new to English, and to school, would be subjected to punishment that is unjustifiable under any circumstance.

Recently I found affirmation in the writings of Roberto Santiago (1995), a scholar who attended Commander Shea as a child. He shares two unforgettable experiences as he sought to understand what made Puerto Ricans special. He writes: "At Commander Shea in Spanish Harlem, a nun told me that Puerto Ricans had no culture. She made me feel stupid for asking the question. ... 'Oppressed,' a priest told me, was what lazy people said they were so they could blame other people for their problems" (p. xiv). These shocking words illuminated an experience I never forgot, but was unable to make sense of until I came across Santiago's experiences. Examining them through the eyes of an adult now evokes memories of missionaries who went to Latin America in search of new Christian converts through unimaginable cruelties.

The next year, I enrolled in the large public school a short distance away from home with capacity for over 1,000 children. At this school, I spent a lot of time as a monitor, assigned to take notes to teachers for their signature. Although it was easy to think that I was made a monitor because I was a good student who would not be harmed by missed instruction, it seems likelier that not being in class made it easier to teach, at a time when most teachers were ill-prepared to meet the needs of the many students who were new to English. After finishing second grade, the New York City Housing Authority (NYCHA) relocated our family to Queens Bridge Housing in Long Island City, near to where my father worked, and where I would attend my third new school in three years. This move marked the beginning of a new chapter in our family life, living for the first time as an American family with my aunts and uncle in an apartment on the Westside near Central Park.

Queens Bridge Housing opened in 1939 and was far more attractive than the dilapidated tenement buildings in El Barrio. The complex was composed of low, six-story buildings positioned to allow sunlight to filter through public spaces between buildings, with neatly manicured grounds that looked like a park. We had our own private world, with stores and play areas where children were safe. We lived near a lovely quiet park by East River, where we went with new friends on what we described as "picnics," carrying blankets and bottles of water. One of these new friends, Viola, remains memorable due to her gentle manner, and also because her mother was Irish and her father Puerto Rican.

At the time, Queens Bridge Housing was the largest public housing complex in the nation, combining both middle- and low-income families. Although Dad was convinced that we were relocated because my parents were stable and responsible adults who met income requirements, I recently discovered that the NYCHA offered alternative housing to "White" middle-income residents to make room for a large number of working-class African American and Latinx families, both to ease the population density of Harlem and East Harlem and to segregate the populations. I suspect that we were among the first of these new residents, and a decade later Queens Bridge was converted into segregated housing, and with it came increased levels of crime and decay that are normative in segregated, low-income public housing. Fortunately for us, we moved out long before that transformation took place.

Just one subway stop away, across the 59th Street Bridge to mid-Manhattan, stood Long Island City, now a major cultural and arts center with many luxury, high-rise apartment buildings. At the time it was a center of heavy industry that included metal works, food processing, woodworking and lumberyards, and stone cutting. The sounds we heard when we left the development were not the sounds we heard on the streets of El Barrio: animated voices of children and adults speaking Spanish (or Italian) and English, sometimes with a musical background. What we heard in Long Island City were the sounds of heavily trafficked roadways and machinery. The move also put a physical and psychological barrier between family and friends who remained in Manhattan, forcing us to interact with others who lived in an area where Spanish was neither heard (nor seen), in public or private spaces. Even so, the move brought some relief to my hardworking parents, Dad at Silvercup and Mom at Eagle Electric Factory. Dad was so close to work that he brought home bread, fresh out of the oven, to our delight. However, the neighborhood where the elementary school I attended was located seemed less populated, with fewer buildings and more private homes. It was very different from El Barrio and a long way from home on a route transited by few pedestrians, near Queens Boulevard.

The two years I spent at this elementary school are memorable because I had my first big performance in fourth grade as part of Thanksgiving Day celebrations. Finding neither photographs nor writings to document what I consider a major "milestone" in my early schooling experiences, I rely on memories evoked by emotions. Assigned the role of narrator, Mom took pride in having me dressed in an authentic pilgrim costume, which I assume my multi-talented Aunt Betsy tailor made for me. I imagine myself standing center stage in the gray, floor-length cotton dress with long sleeves, a white pinafore, and a little cap that fit perfectly. I now wonder if I was assigned that role to accelerate my Americanization, a common practice at the time. However, dream-like memories of volunteering to sing in the cafeteria on days we could not go out to play suggest that I enjoyed performing in public.

I may have been acting out what I saw on children's television programming, or maybe Dad's performances during family celebrations. I was a faithful viewer of *Ding Dong School* (a precursor to *Sesame Street*) and Miss Frances, a credentialed early childhood teacher, whose sweet and gentle conversational manner made me feel as if she were talking only to me. In contrast, the lively *Howdy Doody Show* was more entertaining, fast paced, and louder, like vaudeville for children. The "call-response" opening vivid all these years: "Hey kids, what time is it? It's Howdy Doody time." The high quality of these programs increased exposure to a level of English that exceeded what was accessible at home and in my peer group, and even motivated my public performance. It may sound counterintuitive, but I attribute the level of competence I attained in academic forms of Spanish to a strong foundation in English, made possible by quality children's programming in the home where Spanish remained the language of family life.

Transitions: Coming of Age in the Bronx

Two years after we moved to Long Island City, we moved one more time to the Bronx, a move that coincided with dramatic changes in my physical, social, emotional, and intellectual development, as I was about to begin fifth grade. As a two-income family that had recently acquired a small, mixed-breed terrier, my parents were sent an ultimatum by NYCHA: we either move out voluntarily, or subject ourselves to eviction. Thinking back on it now, my parents did not have much time to be thoughtful about making the important decision to buy our first home, especially a home that came with three rental apartments, and all the maintenance and legal responsibilities that this investment implied. With stable employment, at a time when the city was moving from a manufacturing to a service economy, seven years after arriving, my parents combined $3,500 in savings and secured two mortgages; one for $18,000 (or so Dad wrote in his memoir) and another for $6,000 for a home of our own. The 1931, four-family brownstone on a quiet, tree-lined block in a residential section of the Bronx, made my parents' American Dream come true, but not without hardships. The philanthropic Jewish family who sold the brownstone (I assume from old invitations of fund-raising galas Dad found in the basement), left us an elegant and massive dining room set that accommodated eight comfortably. It was the perfect gift for a family that enjoys gatherings and celebrating special occasions with an assortment of dishes and desserts prepared from scratch by the best cook I have ever known, my mother. I now appreciate what a remarkable achievement it was to be settled in our own home in one of the most diverse working class/middle-income neighborhoods in the city, in zip code 10459.

Our block was composed of one- to four-family homes, with a few six-story apartment buildings on the corner, where kids of all backgrounds—Jewish, Irish, Italian, African-American/Caribbean, and Puerto Rican—developed friendships and played together outdoors. Right around the corner from our home were the offices of Dr. Solomon, the Chilean Sephardic Jew. What my parents did not know is that plans had been drafted that would strip this integrated neighborhood of its tax base, with the construction of a large middle-income complex known as Coop City. Thus urban planning would change the character of a diverse neighborhood, lower the property value of our home, and isolate us through the new Cross Bronx Expressway designed to accommodate the "White flight" to the suburbs that began in the 1950s as public schools were invaded by children of color, from southern states and from the Caribbean. Our fate was sealed; we would soon become a national symbol of urban decay, and zip code 10459 became home to one of the largest and poorest Black and Puerto Rican communities locally and nationally, an issue that President Jimmy Carter brought to national attention. It was fortunate that I was entering fifth grade and my sociable older brother was starting high school. The twins, delivered by Dr. Solomon, were just beginning grade school, and these changes would affect their schooling experiences. I now appreciate the significant impact that attending public schools in the Bronx in the late 1950s had on my coming of age.

The Bronx was the borough with the largest Jewish community in New York City, close to 50 percent of the total population, and 33 percent of the total student population, but Puerto Ricans would soon displace them as the majority. I am convinced that the presence of Jewish teachers, many with a socialist orientation, elevated the quality of public school education I received, at a time when the great majority of students were also Jewish. Thus, attending public schools in the Bronx in the late 1950s just as I was coming of age played a major role in my academic development. However, as the wise Latina that she was, my mother arranged for another equally important learning experience that complemented the formal education public schools (and peers) provided. Beginning in junior high school and continuing through my college years, mother sent me to stay with family in Puerto Rico during summer vacations. These visits were life-altering experiences at a critical juncture in my social, emotional, intellectual, and cultural development that transformed me into a transnational migrant, more so than any other member of my family. This transnational experience is one that many school-age children experience, but that few teachers are prepared to understand when a dominant White-ethnic-class establishes the norms for the great majority of children and youth (and adults) who sustain emotional, cultural, and intellectual (in my case) ties across national boundaries.

Through these experiences, I forged strong connections to family and heritage, and developed a complex identity shaped by lived experiences with many different others. Getting to know the many relatives on Mom's side of the family (several teachers and police officers among them) strengthened my sense of self, and forged new emotional ties to the Spanish language that is our common bond. Although affective bonds to Spanish existed with elders in New York, the language I inherited from my parents was also rapidly taking second place to English in my social and educational worlds. Being fully immersed in island culture also made transparent differences in the way we lived culturally in Puerto Rico and in New York, bringing into focus my own subtleties (and conflicts) in values and practices, as someone who was shaped by both.

Moreover, I studied French at a time when informal exposure to Spanish intensified heightened consciousness of similarities and differences between the two, strengthening both. It is of no minor significance that schooling experiences in the Bronx paved the way to a postsecondary education at a time when fewer than 2 percent of Puerto Ricans had access to a college education, and why my name remained exotic on campus during my college years.

With three income-producing rentals, the unfamiliar and intimidating role of landlord left my parents little time to worry about educational problems affecting their children; they trusted schools to teach us what we needed to learn. Although most of my teachers from grade school to high school were Jewish, my sixth-grade teacher at PS 66X, Mrs. Holstein, remains the most memorable to this day. Sixth grade is a critical transition in our schooling, and in Mrs. Holstein's class I recall research projects that reflected a strong academic curriculum and an emphasis on music. I was so school-oriented that I asked my parents to buy me a Remington typewriter (and a red coat) with insurance monies awarded from an unusual car accident at a yield sign that left my aunts and grandmother seriously hurt. I can only assume that I impressed my teacher when I submitted major assignments typed on my new Remington typewriter. I remember (and Dad did also) the pride I felt during our final assembly program when I received an award for academic achievement and attendance along with a classmate, John Acompore, whom I got to know years later as a respected professional, honored for his contributions on behalf of English Language Learners by the State Association for Bilingual Education, before his passing. I cannot help thinking that Mrs. Holstein made sure that two vulnerable students in her class would not meet the same fate that the great majority of Puerto Rican and Italian students met in the public school system, much of it based on linguistic and racial discrimination.

I have vague recollections of comments written by Mrs. Holstein on my report card in reference to the results of the required IQ test, a score in the 80s or "moron" level, at a critical transition when a teacher makes the decision to act in the interest of a vulnerable student. I assume that Mrs. Holstein challenged a score that was inconsistent with what she knew of me as a serious, hardworking student who contributed to class discussions, and was never late or absent. Advocating on my behalf, she removed a potentially serious impediment to my schooling that other institutional agents might not have been so quick to dismiss, given the tenor of the times: "The evidence indicates that the majority of Puerto Rican children here are so low in intelligence, that they require education of a simplified, manual sort . . . for they cannot adjust in a school system emphasizing the three R's. . . . Puerto Ricans are adding greatly to the already tremendous problem of intellectually subnormal school retardates of alien parentage" (*Report of the Special Commission on Immigration and Naturalization, of the Chamber of Commerce of the State of New York*, 1935; quoted in Zaidi, 2010, p. 227).

In addition to feeling supported by a caring teacher, during those important years of schooling I never doubted that my mostly Jewish classmates took a genuine interest in me, my cultural upbringing, and my heritage, even if peers (now third-generation immigrant Jews) never quite understood why my parents were so strict and overprotective. I felt neither marginalized nor excluded because I spoke Spanish at home, although I recall a number of occasions when I was told that I was "different" when I mentioned being Puerto Rican. However, I did feel different because I was one of the few, and occasionally the only, Puerto Rican in my peer group, and clueless as to why, but I assume Mrs. Holstein knew why. These failures would eventually include my street smart, rebellious older brother and younger sister. Trying to make sense of our different experiences has not been easy, even though my three siblings all became accomplished adults through pathways and opportunities they crafted for themselves, as adults.

In junior high school, I was placed in the orchestra and glee club, in the more challenging, low-exponent classes. I now attribute this placement to Mrs. Holstein's written evaluations of my potential, which I believe changed the course of my life. Given the opportunity to study a foreign language, beginning in grade seven, I chose French. Spanish was not a foreign language to me, and I was unmotivated to study Spanish with teachers who spoke it with an English accent. It is possible that I was smitten with French because, as teachers liked to say, French is a language of world prestige. Thus I learned to read and write in French before doing so in Spanish, publishing a brief poem in French in a school magazine. I am now confident that these experiences heightened my consciousness of the different symbolic media that I was exposed to, and allowed me to take notice of similarities and differences between French and Spanish. In effect, in studying French I gained consciousness of and improved my knowledge of Spanish, in the same way that I gained consciousness of other differences (and similarities) I encountered, because we always see ourselves in relation to what we are not: the "other."

In the ninth grade, we were expected to apply for specialized high schools, and I followed the crowd. I applied for, took a competitive exam, and gained admission to the High School of Music and Art, one of the city's top schools in the performing arts. Spending three years in the orchestra and glee club, with exposure to music theory and practice in reading music notation, led to this accomplishment. However, unable to excel at the violin without private lessons, I enjoyed singing and developed my "alto" voice from being in the chorus, which is how I managed to pass a rigorous written exam and dared to sing "Count Your Blessing" in front of a panel of three judges, without formal training. My father's love of music (he, too, sang harmony or *segunda voz* in musical groups in Puerto Rico), nurtured this passion at home. Regrettably, after a week at Music and Art, I transferred to my local high school because I feared the long, solo commute to Manhattan from the Bronx, and because no one advised me otherwise. However, when I registered at James Monroe (my local high school), a conscientious guidance counselor (Mrs. Brosius) placed me in the honor school as a transfer student from an elite school. Thus, in my high school years I continued to benefit from a two-track system that worked against the great majority of Puerto Rican students, and that prepared me for an academic diploma and a competitive college admission process, as I will explain.

I remained "exotic" as the only Latinx student in the honor school, and learned to become competitive academically, fearlessly taking on a few "arrogant" males who enjoyed displaying their knowledge. However, unlike my peers, I had no academic help at home, nor did I ever consider securing the assistance of a paid tutor. Even so, I managed to attain an 86.4 average in my penultimate semester, with a 90 and 95 in biology and chemistry, passing Regents Exams with honors. English (literature, composition, and language study) was my poorest subject, one I never had the opportunity to study formally as someone who spoke English as a second language, even though I excelled in the interpretation of English literature. Overhearing peers say that they could not go home with anything less than 90, I thought of my parents' pride at knowing that I was doing well in the honor school. Helpful classmates oriented me through the college application process, guiding me to select and apply for admissions to Queens College, knowing of my interest in studying psychology. Queens was and still is considered among the top four-year colleges of the new CUNY system at a time when admission was competitive. This policy worked against the large majority of African American and Puerto Rican students in the system, who would challenge and end it by 1972. And so, my name continued to be "exotic" in my new campus home, where I was one of possibly two Carmens on campus.

I recall vividly my first year on a beautiful, spacious campus that was the closest I would come to going away to college, but where I felt lost without the support of my high school peers. Strolling around the campus, I paused to listen to two young men who seemed to rehearse singing with guitar accompaniment at the back of a building, eventually recognizing them as the musical team of Paul Simon and Art Garfunkel on the verge of fame. That first year, I experienced disappointment that the experimental psychology program I signed up for was not the program I had imagined; eventually settling on Anthropology and Sociology with guidance from new friends. I studied under Hortense Powdermaker, a close friend of Margaret Mead, both of whom engaged in anthropological fieldwork in exotic places that I did not find interesting. Years later, as a doctoral student, I discovered the power of anthropological research in urban schools and communities to inform my work as an educator. I decided on comparative literature as my minor, motivated by reading Luigi Pirandello's *Six Characters in Search of an Author*, a play that has had a profound and lasting effect on my thinking (and creativity). Regrettably, I took Biology that last year at Queens, a course I loved, but too late to make a difference to my plans.

I made two new friends that first year at Queens: Sharon in Freshman English and Lee from hanging out in the cafeteria. Lee introduced me to a group that included males from Latin America who came to study English in the School of General Studies. This was the first time I encountered college-educated Latinx people, and they were charming! Lively, funny, and socially savvy, they captivated me with their experiences living in the United States, even as they offended me with their not so kind views of "American" women, which I was too timid to challenge. Unlike the working-class peers I interacted with in high school, these young men were cosmopolitan, with the stance and stamp of privilege. Yet, despite our different class backgrounds, what we had in common was cultural: the Spanish language, in its infinite varieties and accents that marked national origins as diverse as Colombia, Ecuador, Spain, Venezuela, and Puerto Rico.

This first exposure to the Spanish of the Americas remains memorable. Equally memorable was a brief encounter in which my Nuyorican Spanglish elicited a sotto voce response I have never forgotten: "Que prostitucion del idioma" (literally, "What a prostitution of the language!"). I never verbalized my reaction, but neither did I forget. Heightened consciousness of how class privilege works through language, even among Latinx people, fueled the will to learn. Many years later, I gave a talk in Puerto Rico, and a high-level bureaucrat from the Department of Education (DIP) came up to thank me for my presentation, expressing pleasure and surprise that I did not speak as Nuyoricans who omit final consonants or substitute l's for r's. I was pleased to hear of my "progress" but dared not offer an explanation of the origins and varieties of Puerto Rican Spanish to a well-respected educator who was expressing the limits of her sociolinguistic knowledge, rather than class privilege.

I also confronted rejection in Puerto Rico among some in my cousin's circle of friends, who judged a Spanish that was intertwined with English as a deliberate rejection of my Puerto Rican identity, when it was a reflection of adaptation to life in New York. I was ignorant of the fact that Nuyoricans (also Diasporicans) offend islanders when they act as if they have forgotten how to speak Spanish, after a few short years in New York, which some do. With heightened sensitivity to the role of Spanish in the formation of our national identity, I resolved to develop and strengthen the use of my native language.

I made a hasty decision to study in Puerto Rico after completing my first year at Queens College. In the end I lost a year of study because none of the courses I took at the new branch of Inter-American University were deemed equivalent to those needed to meet distribution requirements at Queens. The courses I took at this branch of a respected university were lacking in the academic rigor of those offered at the University of Puerto Rico or at Queens. The only course that seemed appropriately challenging was the basic Spanish course, where I earned a B, when most of my peers had lower grades. I lost another year to mending a broken heart, which set me back two years when I returned to my studies at Queens, now with a clarity of purpose to a campus that no longer seemed intimidating. Although I completed my degree, I deprived my proud parents of attending my first college graduation, because those who began this journey with me were no longer on campus.

Having neither guidance nor knowledge of what to do next, I graduated from Queens College in June of 1968 with a major in Anthropology/Sociology without having planned my next move, which should have been graduate studies in Sociology or Social Work. Although I was inclined toward the helping professions because that is what my parents did all their lives, I felt lost until my statistics professor—Barry Zamoff, co-director of the Upward Bound Program—offered me a position as mentor and instructor to the mostly Latinx high school students in the program. I did not fully appreciate that the intense and extensive exposure to island culture at a critical period in my development strengthened both parts of the person I am by circumstances of birth and history. I embraced a destiny that gave me the gift of being bilingual and the possibility of being biliterate, but what I could not anticipate at the time was that in developing my biliteracy and bilingualism, I had created unanticipated opportunities and a future unimaginable to me at the time, which I describe in Chapter 3.

Part Two

Learning to Teach

Learning to Teach Children

My path into teaching had fewer obstacles than those encountered by other Latinx people. This was due to the activism of local community and student movements, which challenged educational policies and practices that were having a devastating effect on the lives of children of African American and Puerto Rican origin. These groups constituted the majority of the public school population from the 1950s through the 1970s. Having neither the guidance of helpful peers, nor the benefit of college counseling on how to prepare and apply for graduate studies in Anthropology and Sociology, I was awarded my degree in June of 1968 and remained on campus, as instructor and mentor in the new college preparatory program directed by my statistics professor, Barry Zamoff. A year later, an esteemed colleague in the program, David Forbes, informed me of a new program that was recruiting and training Puerto Rican teachers, and he encouraged me to apply.

The stars were all aligned: New federal funding through Title VII of the Elementary and Secondary Education Act (also known as the Bilingual Education Act) encouraged experimentation with dual language instruction and bilingual teacher preparation and development. Looming on the horizon was a class action suit by Aspira of New York on behalf of the 70 percent of Puerto Rican students who had been dropping out of school. This lawsuit would eventually make accessible instruction in Spanish for Spanish-speaking American citizens who were new to English, through a court agreement known as the Aspira Consent Decree. At that moment I knew that I was destined to become a bilingual educator, as the frustrations and hope of a community that had been demanding change for decades had become a reality:

> Efforts have been made to change the attitudes of teachers toward their Puerto Rican pupils (e.g., Trips to Puerto Rico and seminars to discuss mutual problems), but they have been ineffective. It may be more important to staff schools with Puerto Rican teachers and to introduce Puerto Rican culture into the curriculum and textbooks than to try to change attitudes.
>
> Margolies, 1968, p. 1

Now, after more than a decade of summers in Puerto Rico, I had developed confidence in my ability to teach children in childhood education bilingually. I met the requirements of a new community-oriented program of the New York City Board of Education, the "Recruitment and Training of Puerto Rican Teachers (RTPR)," that prepared college graduates who were bilingual to meet provisional certification requirements. In June of 1969, I began my formal preparation through an alternative pathway into teaching, the Intensive Teacher Education Program (ITEP) of the City University of New York. ITEP was fashioned after the National Teacher Corps program that recruited college graduates who were committed to teaching "disadvantaged youth" (see Othaniel Smith, 1969) as a form of community service (Cordasco & Sanjek, 1969; Travieso, 1975). As director of Teacher Corps in New York City (and also Puerto Rican) Travieso explains: Teacher Corps "helped the cause of bilingual education by establishing demonstration projects throughout the US to address the educational needs of Puerto Ricans and encouraged the institutions of higher education to revise, redesign and create new training models" (1975, pp. 129–130).

The Intensive Teacher Education Program (ITEP) of the City University of New York is a sharp contrast to what we know as Teach for America (TfA), the first of the alternative pathways that emerged in the late 1980s, and the New York City Department of Education Teaching Fellows Program of 2000, the larger of the two. Both TfA and the Teaching Fellows Program recruit graduates of elite colleges, who commit to teaching for three years in an underperforming school. As I describe in Chapter 5, it is assumed that college graduates who have high grade point averages and do well on standardized tests will succeed in increasing the standardized tests scores of children who are categorized as English learners and who attend high poverty schools.

By July of 1969, I had completed the first two required education courses: Problems and Issues of the Teaching Profession, and Teaching Spanish Speaking Americans in Urban Schools. The second step was passing a language exam administered by the intimidating Board of Examiners that had a reputation for failing applicants who had the slightest of regional or foreign accents, which is why many competent teachers from the south and from Latin America never obtained their teaching credentials in the city. Luckily, I was able to secure a temporary per diem certificate that would allow me to begin to teach bilingually in childhood education straight away. I consider myself an unusual teacher candidate because I came to teaching with a combined major in Anthropology and Sociology, a minor in Comparative Literature, bilingual/biliterate competencies developed through informal learning in a Spanish-speaking home and in Puerto Rico during summer vacations, and a strong commitment to community. I consider this background better preparation for teaching in the public schools where I was needed than could be provided by any formal coursework. At the time, leading scholars agreed that dysfunctional Black and Puerto Rican families were the source of their children's school-related problems, a belief that I knew first hand was wrong.

In October of 1969, I was hired to work in an experimental bilingual school where I faced my first class of students, a destiny I rejected as an undergraduate at Queens College because I did not identify with the majority of education majors I met: nice young women whose primary goal in life was to get married and raise a family, who thus sought careers in teaching, an occupation (not a calling) that fitted being a wife and mother. It offered long summer vacations, many school holidays, a stable income, and health benefits. In retrospect, I consider that my entire life, up until this time, was preparation for this moment, and the two years I lost in completing my Bachelor's degree was part of this destiny.

The "school" that opened its doors to me was not your typical turn-of-the century, large and intimidating school of the sort so common in New York City in the days when large waves of European migrants settled there. The abandoned building that once housed a chocolate factory had been transformed into the school that Dr. Carmen E. Rivera (its founding principal) imagined. She explained this transformation at a 1973 national conference on bilingual education: The loft was converted into a beautiful and functional school, introducing the most modern features in school construction and design such as open-wall classrooms, carpeted floors, and acoustic ceilings, the last two intended to reduce the noise level. This type of physical structure facilitated the introduction of a nongraded type of arrangement and the use of team teaching, two other unique aspects of this special school. In addition to its two-track bilingual program, more than 60 percent of the students were from poor and working-class Latinx families, predominantly of Puerto Rican origin. Forty percent were African Americans from families who valued the opportunity to learn Spanish. In effect, this new and unusual learning environment conveyed to children from low-income communities just how special they were.

Located in an old Jewish neighborhood that is now mostly Puerto Rican, and a short car ride from where I grew up and where my parents lived until 2002, the building had three large floors with capacity for 400 to 500 children. On the second and third floors we created sixteen classrooms, moving around and positioning large and small cabinets, chalkboards, tables, and chairs. This opened-wall structure worked to my advantage as a new teacher lacking formal clinical practice experience, allowing me the unusual experience of observing how mostly experienced teachers (the great majority Puerto Rican) engaged in professional practice. What I have come to appreciate, after visiting many other schools in the city, is the collegiality and sense of mission that we all had. We were totally committed to creating a caring, inclusive learning community that provided children of working-class families an unusual opportunity to study in a two-track bilingual program.

To this day, learning another language in grade school is a privilege enjoyed by children from more affluent families, who also excel on traditional measures of school achievement. Thus, working-class Latinx children who were born and/ or raised in New York studied Spanish as a second or heritage language along with the grade-appropriate curriculum in English. Recent arrivals from Spanish-speaking countries studied Spanish as a native language, and the required curriculum in English as a second language. The 40 percent who were African American studied Spanish as a Second Language (SSL), the subject I was assigned to teach during grouping for the "language" strand of the curriculum.

This program appealed to Spanish-speaking families as well as those who valued the opportunity to learn in two languages, regardless of their background. A number of the teachers on staff also enrolled their school-age children in the program, diversifying and broadening the range of experiences of all our children. The teaching staff did not rush out at day's end unless we had an appointment or a class to attend, and we gave of our personal time gladly, to plan and write proposals during nonworking days to assure that our students had access to the best resources and services available. Throughout my years as a public school teacher, I never found another school that matched the gem of a school that 211 was in those early years, even though educators with experiences in more traditional schools had a hard time adjusting to the school's open structure and what they perceived as noise, some leaving soon after they were hired.

A Social Experiment: Teaching Bilingually

We were pioneers in every sense of the word, discovering (or inventing) as we were teaching how to enact dual language instruction. The curricula and instructional materials that emerged and evolved from "learning to teach" and "teaching to learn" in two languages were both locally appropriate and suited to the goals we envisioned. It was not until 1974 that the Bilingual Education Applied Research Unit (BEARU) at Hunter College developed learning objectives and assessments for content area instruction in Spanish. This was hard work, but joyful, collaborative work under the inspirational leadership of a true visionary, Dr. Carmen E. Rivera, whom I have come to appreciate more with the passing of time, and who never received the recognition she deserved.

My first challenge was to get used to teaching in Spanish as a Second Language (SSL) within an instructional model that required 50 percent of instruction in the child's primary language and 50 percent in the child's "second" language. However, the dual language model we followed was carefully thought out, and gradually phased in to allow all of us to adjust to a language policy that the open-wall structure of the school made easy to monitor. Teaching SSL to English-dominant Latinx children from Spanish-speaking homes, I was teaching what we refer to today as Spanish as a heritage language, possibly more challenging than teaching Spanish as a new or foreign language. Teaching Spanish as a heritage language evoked personal memories of being disparaged and humiliated for speaking Spanglish, or Nuyorican Spanish, both in New York and in Puerto Rico. Spanglish, or Nuyorican Spanish, is a form of English and Spanish that emerged in New York City as the children of Spanish-speaking migrant families adjusted to living in a city where English is the language of public life, and where Spanish is the language of intergenerational homes. However, these are also families that sustain contact with the island of Puerto Rico. As sociolinguists explain, in situations where two or more languages are in constant contact, new language varieties emerge through a natural process of coexistence. Such is the situation in Latinx communities in New York (Pedraza, 1987; Zentella, 1997), which was home to the largest of the Puerto Rican communities stateside and the world, until the last decade. Urciuoli (1999) theorizes that children and youth of Puerto Rican origin who sustain contact with the island of Puerto Rico, as is common in New York City and as I did growing up, do not simply develop language varieties that reflect the influence of English and Spanish. English and Spanish are, in fact, so intertwined that they represent one language system, and, I would add, a reflection of the political status of an island that is neither an independent nation nor a state. As Zentella (1997) explains, we need to understand the conditions that give rise to variation in uses of language and literacy—meaning, how they are influenced and shaped by the larger political, socioeconomic, and cultural forces. As a bilingual professional, I have heightened consciousness of the need to avoid code switching in my role as educator, in formal institutional settings. However, during casual conversations with friends and family, I engage in code switching as an expression of solidarity and friendship.

Thus, I brought heightened sensitivity to teaching SSL, with the challenge of broadening a child's experiences of using Spanish in a way that is enjoyable rather than humiliating and intimidating. To this day, teachers are not being prepared to understand what are normal processes of simultaneous language development and usage in social spaces where two or more languages come into contact over a period of time. This lack of preparation affects the quality of reading instruction these children receive, as Moll and Diaz (1980; Moll, Estrada, Diaz & Lopes, 1980) conclude via dramatic videotape evidence that shows differences in reading instruction that children receive in English and Spanish.

My second challenge was to find an identity as a bilingual teacher. I began experimenting with different ways of being a bilingual teacher in my first two years. The only model I had up to that time was the teacher I adored from the distance of a TV screen, but on *Ding Dong School*, Miss Frances did not speak Spanish! Unfamiliar with the world of education as a bilingual professional, I found comfort in being surrounded by colleagues I was privileged to study from a distance. I observed how experienced teachers from Puerto Rico and Cuba used Spanish to teach; their distinctive Spanish accents and ways with words. Similarly, I witnessed creativity and inventiveness by young teachers, schooled in New York, as they went about their teaching day. Never had I been in the presence of so many bilingual professionals in my years of schooling, and unimaginable as colleagues. Years later, I would come to understand what a powerful and unusual experience this was. As a novice teacher, I was learning to teach in a "community of practice" as Lave (1996) describes, in a "borderless classroom," a metaphor that would take on new meaning years later, as I will explain.

And so, imitating colleagues in my visual field, I tried on different identities, from a traditionalist schooled in Cuba, Puerto Rico, Ecuador, and Panama, to more "progressive" colleagues who had been schooled stateside, and who engaged children in performance and arts-based education. By the third year, and like a character in Luigi's Pirandello's (1921) influential play, *Six Characters in Search of an Author*, I authored a "character" that fitted me at the time: someone who grew up watching children's programming, and who was profoundly influenced by Miss Frances, *Howdy Doody*, and my dad's performances. I enjoyed singing popular songs from the new *Sesame Street* program as we danced around our space (not a classroom in a traditional sense) and undertook expressive (sometimes deliberately exaggerated) readings of stories. The anthropologist in me kept the gaze fixed on the children, first scanning, then honing in to observe how individual children responded to my words and actions. I risked writing words backwards in the morning news to check for attentiveness to and comprehension of a string of letters and words that is typically lost when activities become routine.

Once children as young as first grade caught on to my game, they carefully studied what I wrote, and searched for where I tried to trick them, delighting in the moment when they could correct their teacher. Now I had a better reason to make this game increasingly challenging, to see how far I could push. Years later I shared my morning news routine with bilingual and non-bilingual teacher candidates in my courses, but it fell flat. Extracted from the original practice setting where it was embedded, it simply was not the same. Passing down verbal knowledge of practice from one setting to another requires consideration of the many invisible influences on it, as I explain in Chapters 5 and 6.

I also studied individual children carefully as they participated in class discussions and when they worked independently, writing or reading. I observed whether their gaze was distant/blank or focused, what their body posture suggested (slouched, head down), and how they moved their bodies, always in search of indicators that signal a reason to intervene. I looked for signs of nervousness, frustration, and other potentially impedimental responses to instruction, while remaining mindful that young children sit for excessively long periods of time in many schools and so might be agitated simply by being denied activity. Following my instincts, after observing patterns of behavior in one particular child who became seemingly nervous when participating in class, for example hand wringing and shortness of breath, I had an illuminating conversation with her mother at an opportune time. As a result, I learned a very valuable lesson (more like a reminder): influences on learning extend beyond the walls of the classroom. In this instance, I discovered that the child had been a "blue baby," as the mother explained in Spanish, born with the umbilical cord wrapped around her neck, and validating my observations about her manifestation of trauma.

Years later, I would remember this little girl when reading an entry by a horrified undergraduate who witnessed a first grader being forcefully removed from his class, and literally dragged to the principal's office, kicking and screaming. Conferring with that school principal on the disturbing situation, I learned that the number of children in the neighborhood suffering from what she called fetal alcohol syndrome was on the rise. I felt uninformed as an educator and assumed that teachers would also be ill prepared to know how to deal with or, preferably, avoid these moments. I shared this information with a senior professor in Special Education and with the teacher candidates in my literacy courses out of concern that the research-based practices that I encouraged, such as environmental print, could have the opposite effect on some children from what we intended.

Problems that are more common in low-income communities are likely to be misread or misunderstood by uninformed, and even well-intentioned educators. Being an educator requires sensitivity to how our actions affect those we encounter in our classrooms, be they children or adults, and observation remains one of our greatest tools. There is no instrument that can substitute for a sharp observer who is able to put knowledge into practice in the exercise of professional judgment. As an educator, I value both observational and written forms of embedded assessments of children and adults, and consider it a moral issue that we have come to depend on the seeming neutrality of tests to make professional judgments about what children (and adults) know and feel. This is definitely an issue that teacher preparation programs must address through course work or school-based professional development, even as high-stakes assessments are increasingly imposed on teacher education students themselves, and in turn on their professors, who are presumably responsible for their scores.

Accepting the teaching position in a dual language school also came with the ethical responsibility to develop the capacity to use Spanish appropriately in my new role as "teacher." In the open-walled structure of the school, I was both actor and spectator, observing fluent models of professional Spanish with the distinct accents (and melodies) of the Spanish spoken in Puerto Rico, the Dominican Republic, Cuba, Ecuador, and Panama. I suspect that my colleagues had little awareness of the important contributions they were making to my biliterate development in those early years of teaching. Neither students nor colleagues suspected that I compensated for my uncertainties when writing and speaking Spanish as a teacher, by spending hours rehearsing and writing the basic vocabulary and questions I needed to teach on a weekly basis. Eventually, I took special pride in being able to increase the amount of time I was able to sustain speaking in Spanish, without switching to English or mixing the two. Thankfully, alert supervisors noticed and complimented me on the creative ways in which I embedded Spanish into routine activities. Dr. Rivera's overall assessment of my teaching in 1974 included the following praise:

> Your use of Spanish was done in a very natural, authentic way. Children counted in Spanish, referred to sets (conjuntos) and subsets. Children listened and correctly repeated again in Spanish. . . . Your forte appears to be an interest in

what you are doing, an ability to make the teaching learning process a worthwhile meaningful and educational experience for our children, as well as a commitment and loyalty to what we are about—teaching bilingual and non bilingual children bilingually. You are a valuable member of our team.

My greatest inspiration for being the best teacher I could be, and what brought me great joy, was (and remains) the children. I was captivated by the smiling faces and inquisitive eyes of innocent children, who greeted me every morning with a smile, eager to learn and trustful (as were their parents) that I would teach them what they needed to learn to do well in school. I loved how they noticed small details of my attire, my makeup and hairstyle. If they could notice these details, surely they could notice differences between the shapes of letters and words, so important in developmental reading. How they made me laugh in their playful use of language, sometimes brightening a day that may not have had a bright beginning. As a teacher I was positioned to make a difference in the lives of children placed at a disadvantage simply because they came from a home where Spanish was the language of intergenerational family life, and because a busy workweek leaves caregivers little time to accompany young children to the public library. Every minute of the instructional day remains a precious commodity that is not to be wasted in schools in low-income communities, certainly not on lining up or copying drills from the board.

I spent seven years in the classroom, working my way up from fourth grade to a kindergarten-first grade Bridge Class (an innovative feature of the program) because my supervisors thought I would make a good early childhood teacher. Although I initially resisted the idea, it turned out that they were right. I enjoyed teaching children of all ages, but I especially enjoyed watching little people grow and blossom before my very eyes, especially the more fragile ones I knew needed a little more time and nurturing to grow in confidence. As I began to focus on my Master's Thesis, I became increasingly curious about the impact of an instructional model in which students were being exposed to developmental reading in both English and Spanish.

With assistance from my advisor at Lehman College, I designed an investigation titled "A correlation study of the relationship between the measured achievement increment in second language reading with prolonged exposure to bilingual instruction." This longitudinal study was designed to test Malherbe's leveling off hypothesis (cited in Paulston, 1974), using test scores of students who attended the school over a full six years. The leveling off hypothesis predicts that it is only in the upper grades that abilities in both languages level off, and that is precisely what my data supported. However, there were marked gender differences, with girls outperforming boys, validating findings of reading achievement studies at the time, which remain true to this day.

More importantly, findings validated the effectiveness of our new, experimental dual language model on reading in English and Spanish. Just as I completed my Master's Thesis, the American Institutes for Research (AIR) embarked on an evaluation study of the effectiveness of bilingual education programs that included our dual language school among the thirty-eight programs that comprised the sample. In contrast, this national study of a new experimental instructional approach found no differences in the performance of students of Spanish background enrolled in bilingual instruction and those enrolled in all-English classrooms, suggesting to me a political motive. Regrettably, in February of 1977 I had neither the time nor the energy to prepare a manuscript for publication, never making public timely findings that my advisor found so compelling. I left the classroom that seventh year, having accepted a position in a new Title VII Bilingual Teacher Training Program (BTTP) directed by Professor José A. Vázquez-Faría at Hunter College, to begin a new episode in my life as an educator, thanks to the parent of one of my second graders, Professor Migdalia Romero.

Social Experiment: Bilingual Teacher Training

From February 1977 to June of 1988 I worked closely on the BTTP with Professor José A. Vázquez-Faría, my immediate supervisor and director of various federally funded projects and programs, and Professor Migdalia Romero, now a colleague and a friend. From 1980 to 1988, I was instructional coordinator of the New York Multifunctional Resource Center (Title VII ESEA), one of nineteen national technical assistance and support centers funded to address the educational needs of language minority students. My primary responsibilities included planning, designing, and coordinating professional development activities focused on the education of American citizens who resided in homes and communities where language variations of English and other languages were spoken in their home and communities. These activities led to collaborations with staff from the National Clearinghouse for Bilingual Education (NCLB) and Center for Applied Linguistics (CAL), based in Washington DC, to organize activities on the integration of language and content instruction in the school curriculum and in the preparation of teachers. In the early 1980s, I worked directly with some of the leading scholars in an interdisciplinary field of study, who engaged in basic and applied research on instruction in English that is culturally and linguistically responsive to the needs of children and youth identified as English learners or Language Minority Students. Among the scholars who shaped my understandings of English language development through a content-based approach are Anna Uhl Chamot, Michael O'Malley, and Gil Cuevas.

As each three-year cycle came to an end, a new one was proposed, each one building on the last. Thus the Bilingual Teacher Training Program was followed by the Bilingual Objective-Based Teacher Education Program, which was subsequently followed by the Hunter College-CW Post Bilingual Education Service Center, each one broadening our service area to include the four major regions of New York State: New York City, Long Island, the mid-Hudson Region, and Western New York, a region that includes Buffalo. The broad range of students served included the national origin minority children who belong to Tribal Nations, and who live on isolated Indian reservations, where they attend under-resourced schools. The reservation I visited was on a barren and isolated stretch of land near Buffalo. These first Americans were one of four major national origin minority groups that we addressed through activities of our federally funded center, but the great majority were American children of Mexican and Puerto Rican origin, from Spanish-speaking homes.

Officially, I came to work as a Curriculum Specialist, Instructor and Teacher Trainer. My preparation to engage in curriculum development was lived experience, primarily as a classroom teacher, abetted by brief consultant work with the Bilingual Education Applied Research Unit (BEARU) at Hunter College in 1976. Funded by the Ethnic Heritage Act, BEARU developed modules for teacher trainers to assist in the preparation of teachers in multicultural social studies in childhood education. I explored a new field of study that I found more exciting than intimidating, and looked forward to discovering how to work as a teacher trainer and provide on-site support to program participants in schools in East Harlem, in the same neighborhood where I attended my first two years of school. Returning as a professional whose only experience involved a unique model of bilingual education, I developed a broader understanding of the range of programs that develop under different conditions, concluding that we must always attend to the particularities of each setting, rather than talking in generalities of programs or instruction. It is precisely this complexity that makes teacher preparation so challenging. However, at the time, the most challenging (and intimidating) part of my new assignment was teaching adults as an adjunct instructor.

In the new Bilingual Teacher Preparation Program, I taught courses in my department's established "remedial reading" program that combined both bilingual and non-bilingual teacher candidates, as well as courses in the department of educational foundations on the history of bilingual education for teacher candidates seeking certification in a new specialization in Bilingual (Spanish/English) Teacher of Common Branches. Once again, I was charting my own course of study, drawing on lived experiences as an educator, schooling experiences as a student, and an emerging knowledge base generated from the Part C Research Agenda Projects of 1978, a time when the federal government assumed an unprecedented role in initiating and supporting educational research in minoritized communities as a form of social policy. Eventually, I would incorporate major findings that went against the grain of established practice in traditional reading methods courses. According to orthodoxy, assessment of English learners has narrowly focused on oral language and performance on inauthentic tasks. The result has been to underestimate the competence of English learners and an instructional emphasis on decoding and word recognition, as pronunciation problems are equated with poor decoding skills in English (Diaz, Moll & Mehan, 1986; Moll & Diaz, 1980). Further, schools expect students to follow a single developmental model in acquiring uses of language. Developmental models assume a linear progression in learning in which earlier stages will not normally be repeated, and behaviors characteristic of later stages will not precede or appear in the place of later stages (Heath, 1985). Instead, we posited that:

a.   Instruction should be organized as interdisciplinary, six-week thematic units (a preliminary version of coherent instruction).
b.   Growth in literacy is characterized by diversity, not uniformity (Dyson, 1993).

Lacking appropriate and readable professional references (Donaldson, 1978, was a rare find), I prepared detailed "session notes" that synthesized some of the most influential studies on the development of oral and written language, and reading and writing instruction for language minority students. Work that spoke to me as a pedagogue included studies by: McDermott (1977b); Valdes-Fallis (1978); Mehan (1979, 1981); Au and Jordan (1981); Carrasco, Vera, and Cazden (1981); Cummins (1981); Heath (1983, 1985); Wong-Fillmore (1982); Edelsky (1983); Tikunoff (1985); Hudelson (1984); Teale (1984); and Moll and Diaz

(1980). Studying this body of literature would eventually inspire me to organize teaching experiments with classroom teachers who were willing collaborators in the quest to improve children's learning.

As I describe in the next section, I initiated the first of these experiments in 1989, inspired by Heath in a school not far from where I grew up, with a diverse student population about whom I knew very little. The challenge that new (and experienced) educators encounter in low-income communities is the diversity of the student population in local schools, whom most teachers learn to teach through teaching rather than through academic preparation. In contrast, foundation courses in bilingual education promote understandings of the history of U.S. bilingual education program philosophy in relation to models of dual language instruction, and instructional materials in Spanish and English. In both methods and foundations courses, I drew heavily on my unique, lived experiences as a bilingual teacher in a dual language school, infusing meaning into informative readings that graduate students found to be abstract.

Given a new Open Admissions policy, in which any local high school graduate may enroll in a college, most program participants were recent graduates of the City University of New York system of colleges that had opened its doors to African American and Latinx students who were denied access when admission was based on Grade Point Averages and scores on the College Board Exams. The bilingual courses in teacher education were designed to respond to a serious need for teachers who were prepared to teach children whose needs were either not being addressed or were being "misdiagnosed" in traditional teacher preparation. The first bilingual teacher candidates I encountered in the program welcomed the opportunity to address these needs.

The problem I confronted, and that was not of my doing, resulted from combining bilingual and non-bilingual sections. Each group of teacher candidates came to class with very different understandings of the sources of children's reading and writing problems and the type of instruction they needed. For example, the knowledge base I worked from considered portfolio or embedded assessments fairer and more valid indicators of what students understand and are able to do than diagnostic or informal reading inventories. However, inventories are easier to administer and interpret than embedded assessments that require more work on the part of the teacher. It often took a full semester to come to appreciate the substantive content and process of a course designed to address what traditional methods courses in reading and language arts were not designed to consider. Consequently, preparing just one course demanded thoughtfulness in planning and in assessing practice in situ, which is why I typically taught one course per semester. Having just completed a Masters degree as a Reading Specialist, I was far better prepared for being the instructor for Teaching Reading in Bilingual Programs than I was for a course on the Social Foundations of Education, the first two courses I taught in the new bilingual teacher preparation programs.

From the fall of 1977 to the spring of 1988, I was assigned no fewer than eight courses as adjunct instructor. Over these eleven years I preferred combining readings that offered divergent perspectives on a complex subject that I interpreted through the lens of a practitioner familiar with the problems of practice in real practice settings. Initially, I was strongly influenced by an emerging body of research generated through new Title VII Research Agenda Projects that focused on successful practices for teaching "minority language children" (or national origin minority groups) who are U.S. citizens, but who come from homes where languages other than English are spoken. In the New York City of the 1970s, the great majority of children from bilingual homes were of Puerto Rican origin. Thus, planning, implementing, and assessing outcomes of college-credit courses for adults seeking certification in a new specialization in Bilingual (Spanish/English) Teacher of Common Branches was a daunting responsibility that I took seriously because it affected the lives and life chances of vulnerable children.

As members of a caring professional community, my colleagues offered guidance and support by providing sample syllabi and recommendations on worthwhile readings, including relevant articles from the *New York Times* for courses on the Foundations of Bilingual Education. Once again, I was engaged in charting a new course in a new program and a field of study in bilingual teacher preparation that was in its formation. Gradually, I became more comfortable with teaching adults, preferring active learning experiences combined with discussions, rather than lectures, because I was guided by the belief that learning to teach requires putting knowledge into practice. I was fortunate that the great majority of the bilingual teacher candidates I encountered in these early years had been paraprofessionals and came with appropriate dispositions relating to young children, a situation that changed dramatically in my last five years of teaching, as I illustrate in Chapter 5. What these teacher candidates had to learn was the appropriate professional language to characterize their actions.

Student evaluations that first semester generated perfect scores, which was not surprising given that this was a special section designed for grant recipients, the majority of whom were Puerto Ricans. Faculty evaluation for the foundations course rated my teaching satisfactory. I now appreciate a comment that accurately assessed my limited understanding of the sociopolitical context of education at a time when the major achievements of the Black and Puerto Rican communities included public bilingual education and open admissions at CUNY. A faculty observer from the department of educational foundations wrote, "I found Ms Mercado to be quite knowledgeable about the topic of the day's discussion— federal impact on education during the fifties and sixties. If I were to make a recommendation for improvement I would suggest that she familiarize herself with the dialectics between the civil rights movement, and the movement for COMMUNITY control and bilingual education."

With three years of experience, I taught the bilingual section of Studies in Reading and Language Arts. Twenty student evaluations yielded a better understanding of both student and faculty evaluations. The highest ratings on a 5-point scale were for (a) stimulating thinking on the part of students: 4.53; (b) includes worthwhile or informative material that does not duplicate the text: 4.43; and (c) overall teaching effectiveness: 4.40. The lowest rating was for interprets difficult or abstract ideas clearly: 3.87. A well-respected senior scholar, with subject-matter expertise, conducted the course evaluation. He wrote:

> Ms Mercado is a poised, skillful teacher who leads discussion well. She is clear, patient, and knowledgeable, at ease with students. I found the session not only interesting, but I came away with valuable insights for my own classes. We are fortunate in having a young instructor who combines enthusiasm for her work and a valuable background of teaching experience with up-to-date knowledge of important research in language learning.
>
> November 5, 1980

Five years later, another experienced professor observed me teaching the same course, with a similar number of teacher candidates (N=19), and offered distinctly different comments, in content and style. The assessor identifies herself as a "Professor of Curriculum":

> Mercado was well-organized and prepared for this lesson. Students seemed interested, despite the heat. Materials on her desk were to be used the second part of the hour and there was to be a "hands-on experience" to balance the lecture-discussion. The goals for this session were clear and activities related to it. I feel the main weakness of this lesson was pacing.... Introductory materials should have been covered in 5 minutes and the main content of the lesson could begin at 4:30. I commend Mercado for the materials she designed herself. However, I feel they could be better organized.... As I sat through the session I kept wondering why these students are taught separately from others taking an

introductory language arts course, such as 320. In 320, a section is devoted to teaching English as a second language, but the base of the course is teaching "language." That is what these teachers need too. I consider a course like this a blatant segregation of students as well as inefficient use of instructional resources.

At the time, I was taken aback by a comment that was inconsistent with others I had received, but did not take it personally. With multiple responsibilities, I had little time to dwell on it. Returning to it with fresh eyes, I assume it expresses antagonism toward a new bilingual program that departmental colleagues supported enthusiastically, which this colleague may have perceived as being in competition for the same students.

As I began my first year as a bilingual teacher trainer in 1977, I was awarded a Title VII Fellowship to the amount of $7,690 to support my studies at Fordham University as a Bilingual Education Teacher Trainer Fellow in a new field of study that I was literally inventing in and through practice as I went along. By now, this build-the-plane-while-flying process was a familiar experience. In truth, I had not contemplated pursuing advanced studies when I took my leave of absence from teaching school; however, in accepting the award, I was making the commitment to remain in higher education. Completing doctoral courses in bilingual education as I continued to teach graduate courses proved beneficial, as I was now collaborating with local and regional educators on bilingual professional development, and participating in major research initiatives locally (e.g., The Significant Bilingual Instructional Features Study) and nationally (the Center for Applied Linguistic Literacy Studies). Each of these experiences informed one another to the mutual benefit of all, and mostly my development.

In the 1980s I drafted the original design for a Teacher Center on Language Development that eventually became The Language Development Specialist Academy, a unique series of sessions focused on practices grounded in theory and research designed to promote language development among bilingual learners. As the senior member of the team, Migdalia took the lead in directing an activity that met monthly during the school year and over an intense week of full-day sessions in the summer. During these years, I was among a small cadre of engaged, community-conscious Title VII fellows/scholars who crafted new roles and relationships with school districts, to better serve the needs of children who come from homes where languages other than English are spoken (Coballes-Vega, Espino-Paris & Marra, 1979).

Thus, while completing doctoral coursework was instructive, it was the lived experiences of working closely with José and Migdalia in those early years that provided the best preparation I could have as a bilingual educator. José had served as Chief of the Multicultural Division of the National Institute of Education in Washington, DC (1976–1977), where he provided leadership and support in the conduct of scientific inquiry that led to the formation of a new knowledge base on bilingual education and bilingual instruction in the United States. These efforts yielded what are unarguably seminal studies informing bilingual instruction and teacher preparation by the nation's leading researchers. A partnership with Dr. William Tikunoff of the Far West Labs produced two ground-breaking studies of bilingual instruction that combined quantitative and qualitative data (Significant Bilingual Instructional Features Study and Special Alternative Instructional Programs), with New York City as one of five national sites, and I participated in developing instructional implications for these two studies.

In addition, José's network of friends and colleagues was a veritable who's who of leading scholars in bilingualism and bilingual education, nationally and internationally. I had the rare opportunity to get to know invited speakers at local events those first years at Hunter, which led to many publication opportunities, as well as invitations to serve as consultant to the leadership of Center for Applied Linguistics, the Office of Bilingual Education and Minority Language Affairs, and the National Association of Bilingual Education.

As an island-educated Puerto Rican, José had unique expertise with the Spanish of the Americas, which he described in a basic text in Spanish published in the 1980s, loosely translated as "Spanish as a Cultural Link," a perspective that would prove influential in future work. I learned a great deal from engaging in casual conversations with José in Spanish, and appreciated the gentle way he corrected ungrammatical constructions simply by repeating the correct form so I could hear it without further comments. From Migdalia I learned more about the process of working with adult learners, something she had been doing prior to coming to Hunter. I was blessed to have two wonderful mentors and colleagues who ushered me into the academy in one of the largest teacher preparation programs in New York City and in the nation. If it took me eleven years to complete my doctorate, it was, in part, because what I did on a regular basis with my esteemed colleagues was far more compelling and exciting than my doctoral studies, and far more instructive than solitary study when we were writing the script.

Consequently, it took me a long time to identify a focus for my study; my initial interest was studying the metaphoric content of informational prose contained in a major reading and content area series used in Puerto Rico. I wrote several proposals before settling on "An ethnographic study of classroom help with language minority students," building on the work of my advisor combined with my interest in classroom instruction. Data were derived from videotapes of classroom activities, field notes, student and teacher interviews, and examination of the schoolwork of primarily Latinx and Asian-origin students, grades four and five. The three teachers who volunteered were Puerto Rican females with no fewer than three years of experience, and instruction was conducted primarily in English.

The overwhelming amount of qualitative data this study generated took a good two years to organize, synthesize, and theorize. I thought I would never get it done, but I eventually did in May, 1988. The two most memorable aspects of this study were the opportunity (a) to understand classroom life through the eyes of children in the elementary grades; and (b) to work collegially with the teachers in understanding classroom life through their perspective and presenting findings that I considered the shared property of all of us at local and national conferences. This collaborative approach to research and teaching has characterized my work since I began; and I am incapable of working any other way. Even when I appear to work alone, the voices of my invisible collaborators are always present.

Becoming a Teaching Educator

In this chapter, I describe two critical transitions in my professional trajectory as a full-time faculty member in the Department of Curriculum and Teaching, in one of the largest teacher education programs locally and nationally. These transitions include: (a) the vulnerable pre-tenure years, from 1988 to 1993; and (b) the first years as an associate professor with tenure (1994–1999). However, it bears repeating: By the fall of 1988, I had been teaching as an adjunct instructor for eleven years (fall 1977 to spring 1988) and was well versed in the complex process of preparing course syllabi, a legal document that grew increasingly longer (and more intimidating) as new institutional policies were added.

What was challenging and new was teaching with all the institutional responsibilities that full-time faculty is expected to meet. One problem was that the same "advanced reading and language arts" course I had taught for more than a decade was a requirement for pre- and in-service teacher candidates specializing in "remedial reading," childhood education, and bilingual education. Different perspectives guide each specialization on addressing learner differences. In addition, special sections of the course designated as "bilingual" require teaching in Spanish and English, and occasionally these sections include both bilingual and non-bilingual teacher candidates. Discovering challenges I did not anticipate, I was obligated to meet the needs of all, as best I could. I now understand that due to minimal enrollment requirements, sections are either combined or eliminated, and those who registered for these courses should have been informed of these last minute changes. These local institutional influences on practice shape individual and collective experiences of a course, and explain the sense that we all make of these experiences. The problem is that these influences remain invisible in formal and informal assessments of course experiences.

In this chapter and the next, I consider how I addressed an unusual level of complexity carrying a full course load of twenty-one credits a year (or seven three-credit courses) in the bilingual education and reading specializations as my responsibilities increased exponentially in a service-oriented institution.

Therefore, while the focus is primarily on preparing teachers to teach reading and language arts, it is important to understand the complex web of activities in which professional practice is embedded, one that is combined with other institutional responsibilities, including committee work, institutional service, and service to community. Understanding the demands I confronted, my official mentor, the director/coordinator of the reading specialization, offered wise advice this first semester: to be mindful of the need to organize my time to produce one major publication a year, advice that I faithfully followed as someone who by this time knew that teacher education was where I needed to remain.

Course Content and Processes

Even with a heavy workload, I organized highly interactive, writing-intensive activities that I considered appropriate to a course on teaching reading and language arts in which reading and writing are both content and process. By the time I became a full-time faculty member on tenure track, I had developed a repertoire of nontraditional activities that deliberately disrupted familiar structures of participation in preparing teachers to teach and assess language and literacy instruction that, from the beginning, focused on the needs of English learners in high needs elementary schools. Understanding that teaching is a transactional process, I recognized the urgency of knowing how adult learners experience weekly encounters in a college-based methods course that requires them to address theory and research that inform and shape practice. I also offered real-life examples of practices I adapted from the professional literature to demonstrate alternative approaches to the teaching of reading and language arts, and shared my work-in-progress for our mutual benefit.

Although in these early years the term "community of practice" was not in my lexicon, it has been manifest in my practice, which has been characterized by collaboration and mutual assistance (or reciprocal teaching and learning). I now understand that this disposition may have been shaped by years of working in professional development. This pedagogical approach also explains why I am compelled to make visible the perspective of adults who share these experiences with me, through anonymous excerpts of session logs and other reflective writings completed during each session. In 1991, I made a first effort to co-author a manuscript with a pre-service teacher in the "advanced" reading course. Although we were not able to go beyond first drafts, the manuscript was published as part of the conference proceedings of the National Association of

Bilingual Education in 1992. In this narrative excerpt, Dawn gives a sense of the experience of learning to teach reading in the spring 1991, the semester that marked the end of my third year as a full-time instructor.

> I entered the first session of class expecting it to be similar to other graduate courses that I had taken, prepared for what would be two hours of rigorous note taking. Instead we were greeted by a professor who seemed warm and expressive, who wanted to allay our fears by presenting us with a mnemonic of her name.
>
> (**M**odeling practices; **E**ngaging in talk and writing to enlighten/clarify thinking; **R**eflective/analytical teaching; **C**aring learning community; **A**ssisted/mediated performance; **D**oing and discovering; **O**rganization and planning.)
>
> Each letter represented a portion of her philosophy about teaching and learning. She encouraged us to ask her questions and made us aware of two learning exercises. The first involved students summarizing relevant articles for the class. This divided the responsibility for transmitting information and allowed students a more active role in learning. ... Students benefit from this type of activity because learners sometimes learn more from their peers than from their teachers. Another exercise was the writing of logs, to be completed at the end of every session. These logs recorded questions on coursework, discussions and personal growth. They created an open arena for honest communication between students and teachers. Occasionally during the semester our professor would photocopy portions of our logs for discussion. This was done anonymously. In allowing time between the writing and the rereading, we reflect on what was happening, what we were learning and how our ideas were changing. In this manner, we were able to assess growth in ourselves and in our peers.
>
> Our coursework required that we complete two large projects. Normally in graduate courses students work on projects independently. Projects are handed in at the end of the semester, graded and returned with a minimal of discussion. In our class, a student's work was assessed at various points during the semester. At each session, at least two students discussed their work in progress. We were able to see ideas in the making, as well as all the projects finally coming together ... and derived the benefit not only from our own learning but also from the learning of others. ... Our professor shared her work in progress with us; we saw her learning through doing, and benefitted from her first hand experiences.
>
> On another occasion, our professor began the session speaking in Spanish. Initially we were shocked and a bit nervous, which was evident from our giggles. And as she proceeded to read a story in Spanish, the class became a bit more serious and directed. It was obvious that there were speakers of Spanish who fully understood the story. They followed along and answered the questions at the appropriate time. The rest of the class ... felt challenged by the exercise, trying to use background knowledge of other languages to decipher meaning. It is

extremely disconcerting to feel as if the excitement is passing you by. The point of this activity is to elicit the feelings of a second language learner. We were immersed in an experience that would not have made the same impression had we read about it in a textbook. The feelings of frustration and anxiety . . . were our feelings as we sat while the dialogue progressed without our input or understanding.

Although session logs were initially intended to address the engagement problem that I found disconcerting as a graduate student in education, they proved to be an effective vehicle to building trusting, caring relationships, which McDermott (1977b) describes and Bruner (1996) suggests are fundamental to developing mutual understanding. I needed to learn from the perspectives of those who engaged with me in this journey; they shaped how I organized sessions from week to week, and across the semester, as I read, responded in writing to individual logs, and summarized major themes and common concerns that emerged from reading all the logs. What I learned from each semester's experiences shaped future semesters, and is why I extended the invitation to all participants to co-author a manuscript with me during that important third-year milestone as full-time faculty. Dawn's writing contributes to a historiography of a first semester reading course, as did all who took the class in the fall of 1993. The narrative that follows represents a tapestry of twenty voices.

> We wrote logs every week in class as a reflection of the day. I felt as though I could write what I thought, summarize what I learned and provide you with material to use for assessing my progress . . . useful in an atmosphere where the student feels comfortable enough to share thoughts, ask questions, disagree, and evaluate the activities in the classroom (1). You took the time to make comments on almost all the logs submitted. The read around that we exercised was a good chance for me to individually speak without interruption, at the same time, listen to what others had to say (2). A large portion of the class was spent on debriefing following an experience (e.g., a twenty-minute Spanish immersion experience; reading and answering questions on "Farfie Mardsen," a passage Ken Goodman developed as a teaching tool to illustrate that we are able to answer comprehension questions drawing on our knowledge of English orthography and syntax without understanding the meaning of the passage. This method leads to more active learning (3). I am very happy that a major part of this course focused on teaching literacy to students whose first language is not English . . . I will be studying Spanish in Mexico this summer. Projects that the class did with bilingual learners gave us a chance to get a close up look at some of the things these students go through in schools where instruction is in English (4). I have only taken a handful of graduate level courses, but your emphasis on multicultural backgrounds is the first opportunity for me to really think about how diverse cultures affect the teaching-

learning process. I am actually shocked that that in a NYC college, more classes are not incorporating ethnicity into the course agenda! It seems obvious that you are passionate about what you teach and care about translating the importance of pedagogy to the class (5). Respect for where everyone was, and where he or she is coming from was also a part of the classroom. One of the things I really like about Hunter is the diversity of the students in the classroom. In this class that was used as an asset, for each person had something special to add, and since everyone's past experiences had varied so much, it gave the class more than one perspective in many instances (6). The instructor created mutual respect with the students by letting us somewhat guide her in the material that would be covered in the classroom time (7). My classmates were more cooperative, motivated and thoughtful than in any class I have had thus far. We helped each other out of a sense of caring, professionalism (as was expected of us), and to a certain degree, out of need and solidarity (8). You encouraged us to use all of our resources: colleagues, students, professors, and professional organizations. You also embedded in me to hypothesize, revise, and ask even more questions (9). I came to this course expecting to learn about Informal Reading Inventories and basal series. I had no idea that we would be exploring biliteracy and equity issues in education (10). What made the class most challenging was the newness (11). This was one of the most demanding courses I have ever taken at Hunter, primarily in terms of the time it required. Not only were we expected to be prepared and alert in class, we had to meet with our student subjects on a weekly basis and keep detailed notes on these meetings (12). The process-oriented method that you use is effective in the long run, but has the tendency to make students feel insecure about the learning of content. It was usually after the fact that we were able to see the "whole picture." Perhaps some advance assurance or advisement would aid the students in recognizing that the components of your course will eventually structure a very substantial total approach to the integrated language approach (13). I only have one complaint regarding the class, which is the unorthodox approach that was used in teaching the class. I was continually unsure about my grade until the mid-term exam. I will admit, throughout the course you gave much feedback regarding my concerns (14). You permitted us to really take charge, providing us with an outline to cover and sort, but not limiting us to uniform structure. Although this was tough ... I think that you were encouraging us to take a risk, so that we could develop autonomy (15). My concept of how I learn has changed greatly. . . . I struggled with many questions and ideas. I thought that my not knowing the answers was a result of the instruction not to be clear and defined. I now know that my struggle was my actual learning process. Knowledge is not always handed to you in terms you are familiar with. I was used to being handed material, reading it, comprehending and giving it back in one form or another, for example a test, paper, etc. I now feel strongly that in order for learning to take place a real change must occur in the way we think. In order for change to occur our beliefs must be challenged in such a way that we begin to question and rethink and perhaps modify and/or change our thoughts (16). My descriptive review and later my thematic unit and assessment showed me how little this process had to do with what you wanted and how much it had to do with what I needed to learn (17). One student described the class as a carousel ride. For me this class was like a water slide: it was often slippery, frightening, and uncontrollable. However, it was also exhilarating. (And it's not over yet!) (18). I felt challenged (and required) to carefully evaluate and reflect on everything I heard and read, and interpret its meaning, and put it to use. I believe this process required each student in the class to think quickly and concentrate hard on the material, to give up our "normal" graduate student mode of meeting requirements as a trade-off to real learning and to open to new ideas and modes. This is especially difficult for adult students. A great deal of trust was necessary for me to benefit from this process . . . I can see that other students in the class may not have been so trusting, because of both external and internal factors (19). This class has been extremely challenging for me. Even now that it is almost over . . . I still feel challenged by it. I think this is because I do not feel completely competent to assess a student without using traditional methods . . . I would not say the work was difficult, but I do say the class was difficult because of the amount and kind of thinking that was required (20).

One participant candidly describes her struggles in the course during the spring 1994 semester. She makes a sharp observation that few have grasped, on what some scholars refer to as "presence," more like embodied listening than active listening and associated with building positive relationships of trust, whether with children or adults, because it conveys that what the person is saying is important to me as the listener/"pedagogue." As this pre-service teacher admits, she shifted from resisting to "giving in":

This class has really opened my eyes. . . . During the first session . . . I was very uncomfortable. I remained in this state for a few sessions after that. I cannot recall any one particular incident that was making me feel uneasy—it was the class and how you conducted it. It was very foreign to me. I just wanted to get out of there as soon as I possibly could. I had never experienced the type of writing you were requiring us to do, the expert groups, the overall participation you demanded from us. You weren't just spewing out information to us. . . . You were challenging us to make our own meaning, right there and then in the class—not when we went home. . . . This seemed so alien to me that I guess my reaction was to resist at first. It's not that I've never had open discussions in my classes. . . . It was the way in which we spoke and discussed and the way you listened to us when we speak. I've watched you do it. You focus on the person who is speaking so intently as to totally tune that person in. You totally give them the floor and I think this is very empowering, even for graduate students. We exchanged ideas, thoughts, dissatisfactions, right there in the class as it happened and you put us in situations that forced us to think about what we do in our classrooms. It's hard to explain. I say it was almost a timely reaction to our direct involvement/instruction because if we didn't react or reflect in class, the moment would be lost and the experience would not be our own. [This young woman requested doing an independent study with me the following semester. I still have the tiny piece of paper where she wrote: "I intended to resist you, but you won and I learned."]

Despite the hard work it required of all of involved, I enjoyed the challenge that teaching adults presented, but I also missed teaching children, and needed to act on the reading "problems" of mostly Latinx students in real classrooms. The opening came in the form of a professional article I assigned as required reading in the fall of 1988. A 1985 article by Shirley Brice Heath was both moving and inspiring, and encouraged me to reassess the traditional preparation I had received in the Reading Specialists Program offered at the City University where I completed my Masters degree in 1977. Heath, a former high school teacher turned educational ethnographer, conceptualized literacy as a social practice (rather than as an individual skill), and learning as a social process (rather than knowledge transmission and acquisition), perspectives that guided her work with low-scoring high school students. These students included second language learners and special learners (meaning special education). Preferring to enrich rather than remediate, Heath engaged these students in an unusual form of distant learning that involved the exchange of written correspondence or letters, in days before the technological revolution put electronic forms of communication at our fingertips.

Over time, this long-distance, knowledge-building community enabled students whose abilities were judged on the basis of their performance on standardized reading tests to engage in ethnographic research on language uses in their communities, with a respected scholar and her former student (their teacher). Through their participation in this experience, students were able to describe observations and offer explanations for data they collected. Descriptions and explanations negotiated through written conversations from a distance, over the course of a year led to a sophisticated understanding of how language works, and improvements in students' analytical writing and sense of self. It also produced gains on standardized tests of reading and writing, demonstrating what is possible when we think differently about learning to read and write, as well as about learning to teach reading and writing, in a manner that assumes competence rather than deficits among participants.

Heath's work affected me emotionally and intellectually, such that in my second semester as new assistant professor I assigned her article as required reading, and looked forward to reading comments in weekly logs. Responding to comments by a sixth-grade, middle school teacher (Marceline or Marcy Torres) led to an invitation to visit her classroom. In the fall of 1989, my visit to her class led to a professional relationship that has resulted in an enduring friendship, at the time focused on addressing the "reading and writing problems" of sixth graders who are described as being "very poor at writing." It is this experience that I describe as Teaching Experiment 1.

Teaching Experiment 1: Connecting Communities of Practice

My first impression of the Bronx Middle School was that it looked like a jail. Only later did I discover that fewer than 25 percent of its Latinx and African American students were on grade level in reading, and why the school ranked tenth from the bottom among all middle schools in New York City. I also discovered that it is one of the schools Jonathan Kozol describes his 1992 book, *Savage Inequalities*. Introducing a rigorous inquiry-oriented project that builds on local knowledge was perceived by some teachers as "crazy" or ill-conceived, as it challenges a classic example of what Haberman (1991) describes as a "pedagogy of poverty." Haberman describes fourteen acts that he believes are standard practice in poor urban classrooms: giving information, asking questions, giving directions, making assignments, monitoring seatwork, reviewing assignments, giving tests, reviewing tests, assigning homework, reviewing homework, settling disputes, punishing noncompliance, marking papers, and giving grades. Haberman explains that taken separately, there may be nothing wrong with these activities. Any one might have a beneficial effect. Taken together and performed to the systematic exclusion of other acts, they have become the pedagogical coin of the realm in urban schools. They constitute the pedagogy of poverty, deeply embedded in urban schools.

In contrast, our collaborative inquiry approach would engage sixth-grade middle school students in what Haberman (1991) characterizes as good teaching. Students are involved with:

a. issues they regard as vital concerns;
b. explanations of human differences. "Why are there so many problems in our community?";
c. a focus on big ideas, and general principles and not simply the pursuit of isolated facts;

d.   planning what they will be doing;

e.   applying ideals such as fairness, equity, or justice to their world;

f.   real-life experience, directly, including field trips, interacting with
     resource people, and work and life experiences—followed by thoughtful
     reflection;

g.   redoing, polishing, or perfecting their work; and

h.   reflecting on their own lives and how they have come to believe and feel as
     they do.

Haberman concludes, and we agree, that "good teaching" is a process of drawing
out rather than stuffing in.

The braiding of personal, professional, and community needs proved powerful
when combined with sage advice offered by Heath (1983): "Put ethnography into
the hands of those who will use it to improve their knowledge of what is
happening around them, and they will improve their learning and skills in oral
and written language" (p. 18). What I could not anticipate was how this would
work out with sixth graders in a middle school, who ranged in age from eleven
to fourteen, many repeating first grade because language differences were treated
as linguistic and cognitive deficits.

From the first day I entered Marcy's classroom, it became my refuge and my
training ground as we experimented with a writing-intensive, inquiry approach
that engaged all of us in collaborative teaching and research, an approach that
was also inspired by Woodard (1985). During that first encounter I shocked
students who had initially envisioned me as a bald, Jewish man who wore glasses.
They could not believe that I was a Puerto Rican with a Ph.D. Perplexed as to
why I would want to "waste" time with them as a college professor, one asked if I
was getting paid to work with them, apparently knowledgeable about grants that
some educators receive for special programs. I responded that I did not get paid
for coming to work with them; that I came because I needed to learn from them
in order to teach teachers. I asked the students what they wanted to learn. In the
fall of 1989, their responses were astonishing: "Why are there so many problems
in our community?"—problems such as homelessness, AIDS, violence, teen
pregnancy. Wise beyond their years, these young people understood what
educational researchers sometimes overlook, and what the title of a seminal
article by Moll and Diaz (1987) captures: the importance of "change as the goal
of educational research." With their parents' permission, in teams they organized
based on mutual interest or solidarity, students began searching in earnest for
answers in much the way I do research: by observing, listening, talking to

"authorities," reading informative sources, and keeping a written record of what I do and learn. Long before the end of that school year, they began to transform insecurities and self-doubt into confidence in their capacity to do "college" work, evident in their posture as well as their words.

After we were well into our work, I introduced the idea of presenting at research conferences, because it is part of doing research as a professional. Over the years I applied for and received several small research grants (under $10,000 in total) that would enable us to travel in small groups accompanied by a few adults, when students felt well prepared and ready. By the end of that first year, all had gotten on board. Traveling to conferences by train, we met interesting adults who were curious about our group. We stayed at major hotels and entered new knowledge-building communities where educational professionals and scholars shared their work and learned from their colleagues' projects.

For our first conference presentation, we traveled by subway to Lincoln Center, seeing parts of the city some had never seen because few left the area where they lived. Our first session was accepted at the annual Parents and Reading Conference in December of 1989. In February of 1990, I entered into another knowledge-building community of practice at the Ethnography Forum of the University of Pennsylvania, along with young people whom the Forum director recognized as junior ethnographers. We also attended the National Association of Bilingual Educators in Washington, DC where we spent the night at the Hilton Hotel, visited our local Congress representative, did a tour of the city courtesy of a friend who worked at the FBI, and mingled with "Dr. Mercado's friends." (They refused to address me by my given name out of respect.)

The two parents who accompanied us on this trip also presented on how they experienced the project and shared unsolicited insights on how their children were changing through the experiences we organized. One of the parents revealed surprising insights on how a research project some describe as a "family" was having a positive influence on her son at home: He seemed more cooperative and mature. In general, the experiences fostered the capacity of young adolescent learners to address the serious issues that concerned them, to tell our research story far more eloquently than any of their adult guides were capable of doing. A few said they wanted to speak like me, as an academic, but most spoke in their authentic voices.

Through our experiences, students gained the recognition of prominent scholars who offered encouragement, as Dr. Fred Erickson did, greeting us at the conference and subsequently writing directly to students, boosting their self-esteem. Some scholars spoke directly to me, as Mariane Hedegaard did, while others, understanding the need for professional documentation, wrote to acknowledge that "this kind of work—involving teachers, students and university professors—demonstrates why education must be coupled with dignity, respect and dialogue, and what it can offer when it begins with the political realities of the students, in their communities" (personal communication, Dr. Deborah Britzman, 1990). Over the years, and until the last semester before retirement, the writings of these student ethnographers became required reading in my courses, offering insights and advice to future teachers on the importance of teaching literacy, permanently preserved in written words that travel through time. As the comments of pre- and in-service teachers reveal, the writings of these young scholars proved to be a powerful educator.

This bold experiment, in which educators organized challenging learning environments because they believed in students' capacity to learn, went against conventional thinking in 1989. Students appropriated the tools and practices of inquiry to become self-reliant and self-assured learners capable of paving their own path toward self-realization that schools are unlikely to provide. One male that I know of employed the tools of research to begin exploring the high school selection process by way of having a say in the high school he wanted to attend. Through collective action, adult guides also enabled students to navigate obstacles that controlled and limited their opportunities to learn, to understand that some of the "family problems" that were so affecting resulted from access to a livable wage, in a school where few teachers acted in the interest of students.

In addition, gain scores on state reading and writing exams were well above what was considered a significant increase (4 points), some as high as 30 points. This did not occur because we prepped the students for these tests, but there may have been other factors at play beyond a challenging curriculum that focused on "real life," including increased confidence and self-esteem, which was noticeable in posture, attire, and attentiveness. What I would like to believe is that through our collective efforts we transformed a site of deprivation, a classroom in a school of savage inequalities, into a site of radical possibilities, inspiring others who may never experience marginality, as hooks (1994) theorizes. The experience changed students' relationships with themselves, with others, and with their social worlds. It also changed their adult guides (including parents) as much as those who witnessed public performances and read writings that reflected their authentic voices. Through this experience, Marcy and I are now *comadres*, a word that captures cultural nuances absent in the word "friend." I recently came across a 1969 publication, *Teachers for the Real World*, and I realized just how much Marcy exemplifies the qualities of effective teachers of "disadvantaged" youth that Othaniel Smith (1969) describes (see Figure 4.1), and that the middle school students acknowledged in their descriptions of her.

Although the project led to ten publications, and nineteen presentations at local, national, and international conferences, it is the writings of middle school students that remain a powerful teaching tool, touching past, present, and future educators, as Chapter 5 illustrates. Now mature adults, some remember doing research with "Dr. Mercado," admitting that it brought comfort in challenging moments in their lives. I would like to believe that courageous students from the margins continue to influence a mainstream research community that now seeks to actively sponsor youth researchers nationally and internationally, as the American Educational Research Association did in 2015. I attribute my 1993 promotion and tenure as associate professor to a small-scale initiative that yielded compelling counter-stories, through a smooth braiding of my personal, professional, and community life with the meaningful integration of teaching, scholarship, and service. This was the first time that my parents were brought into my professional world, as curious sixth graders expressed interest in meeting the man (my dad) who dropped me off at the school each morning.

An effective teacher is . . .

- Human.
- Aware of the realities involved in preparing students for the real world.
- Able to structure and supervise situations where learners can engage in useful activity.
- Skillful at bringing together persons of diverse races and classes and keeping the communication process going until differences are resolved.
- Able to learn from the past or to learn from complicated messages conveyed through art and music by being well versed in music.
- Prepared to negotiate interpersonal contracts with students.
- A person a student trusts.
- Able to share valuable knowledge and experience.
- Able to communicate to a broad segment of society, and has knowledge of languages and linguistics.
- Able to understand the students' world.

Figure 4.1 Skills of an Effective Teacher of "Disadvantaged Youth"

It is no exaggeration to say that this project has affected many over the years, especially one graduate student (Patty) who chose to learn to teach in a school not likely to be selected as a site for clinical practice, but that, at the time, could have benefitted from the support. As Patty describes in an unpublished manuscript for AERA (1993), students who became "teachers of teachers" offer insightful and wise advice on being a "good" teacher.

Patty Reflects on the Past and Sees a Future

I was born and lived the first seventeen years of my life twenty miles away from New York City. I grew up in the section of town that was called "down-the-hill," and this term, I later discovered, served as a metaphor about the way everyone thought about the people in my neighborhood. We were the bottom: My elementary school was about 60 percent white, working class (Irish and Italian) and 40 percent African American. It was a neighborhood in transition but I didn't understand that at the time. What was unique about my early schooling was that everyone learned and played together.

When I entered high school, I learned quickly that I was "working class." At fifteen years old I became aware that my education was inadequate. My first nine years of school were easy, too easy. I entered high school thinking that I was a genius. I never had to do any homework and I always received high marks on my report card. However, once I entered the halls of West Orange High that all changed. Due to tracking, I was placed in the top class. What I noticed was that my friends from the neighborhood were no longer in any of my classes, and that I had not learned the same things in elementary school that the other kids had. They had read literature, Shakespeare, taken Algebra, participated in theater and benefitted from all those activities that good schools have. It is this experience, this feeling of not being good enough that gives me the strength and the desire to teach children, those children who because of where they live are condemned to a second rate education.

Before I began this project, I really didn't know where I was going. I had spent the past three years working as a contracts administrator for a television production company while secretly wanting to teach. I first became interested in teaching after I participated in IMPACT, a volunteer program that helped homeless children living in a large hotel converted into a shelter. Once I knew I wanted to work with children, I decided to take a few courses before switching careers. I didn't feel qualified enough to teach with a TPD (Temporary Per Diem) certificate, I wanted some practical knowledge. The first day I walked into the Advanced Reading class I was optimistic. I was looking forward to the course since I had such a wonderful experience in my last reading course. Upon walking into the room, I was immediately confronted by a professor who seemed to exhibit two extremely different characteristics. Initially I saw a kind and compassionate teacher who wanted to help us grow to a higher level of understanding and at the same time an intimidating professor who had unrealistic expectations that I could never meet. I was overwhelmed by the quantity of work to be produced during the semester. The professor announced to the class that this was a special section of Advanced Reading, designed to assist teachers with second language learners in the classroom. ... My purpose for attending this section was to prepare myself for the second language learners I would encounter in my future classroom. The tension I felt became insurmountable as I realized that this class was designed for teachers working in a classroom with second language learners. I began to hear the following: portfolios, assessment, working with four children you were teaching (did these children have to be real?), and THEMATIC UNIT. I began to realize how much I did not know, and of course the idea that I had made a big mistake thinking I could take education courses without being in the classroom. I decided I would go to one more session before I would drop this class. Somehow, the next class calmed my fears; I understood more than I previously thought. I decided to make an appointment with the compassionate yet intimidating professor.

On March 7 I was definitely going to drop; my job lost two positions and their duties were added to my job description. I was very nervous when I went to my professor's office. I burst out my plight about not having enough time to spend in a classroom and I didn't have friends who would help me; I don't know when my whining stopped, but then the professor made me an offer I couldn't refuse. She offered me a chance to help her develop portfolios for her students. It was what happened next that helped me see the light. The professor shared something from a student's journal with me. I read it briefly in her office and it was these words that changed my attitude toward this class. She then asked me to think what I would say to Teddy, and how I would assess his work. It was after reading Teddy's journal that I had a reason to stay in this class.

May 30, 1991

As is evident in this brief narrative, the experience of learning to teach in and through personal and collaborative relationships with sixth graders, aged eleven to fourteen, in a school that really benefits from our presence, is a powerful educator. Years later, the Milwaukee Teacher Education Model that Martin Haberman developed validated what Patty had discovered on her own, that urban teachers should learn to teach in the poorest schools rather than learning to teach under ideal or even satisfactory conditions (Haberman, 2000).

Clearly when we all set out on this journey, we did not know how it would unfold and the different outcomes it would produce. Even so, we were confident that the journey was likely to take us to a better place than the one we left, and it did. In addition to the positive impact our five-year collaborative research had on middle school students, Marcy was offered the opportunity to create a research program in her district. Patty did not have to wait long to find a teaching position where she was needed. I was granted tenure and promotion to associate professor in the fall of 1993, after five years of hard work. Exhausted from a heavy teaching load and involvement in a broad range of professional and community activities, I applied for and was granted a year sabbatical with a half-year salary. I left for Phoenix Arizona in June 1994, beginning a year of much needed renewal and reflection, and conversations with like-minded colleagues and friends in the southwest. I can honestly say that I was reborn in the desert, after adjusting to a topography that was radically different from the tropical island where I was born, and incomparable to the megalopolis where I have lived most of my life.

Living in Phoenix, I had several opportunities to meet with the university-based team from the Study of Community Funds of Knowledge that was now widely recognized as one of the most significant research projects of the last two decades. I first heard about this study in 1989, at the invitational research symposium held in Washington, DC, where the principal investigator, Dr. Luis Moll, presented preliminary findings on learning from participant-observation in the homes of modest-income Mexican families in Tucson, Arizona. The Arizona research team included a teacher-researcher (and doctoral candidate), an anthropologist (Norma Gonzalez), and an educational psychologist (Luis Moll), all bilingual and biliterate. As a bilingual literacy educator, I was compelled to understand community uses of literacy in English and Spanish in local Latinx communities.

I also attended the Whole Language Winter Institute, an annual event organized by Ken and Yetta Goodman, where I experienced a week of intellectually stimulating talks led by an international group of scholars. What remains most memorable to me is that, at this event, I met a group of young scholars (all women) from the University of Puerto Rico (UPR), some engaged in or contemplating doctoral studies at the University of Arizona, as was Carmen Martinez Roldan, now a professor at Teachers College in New York. Most of the Latinx scholars I worked with at CUNY, with few exceptions, were in the social sciences and male. I had the opportunity to visit with Dr. Ruth Vega Saez, an early childhood specialist at the UPR, who was working on her dissertation in biliteracy, with Luis Moll as her advisor. In the short time that I spent with Ruth, we would stay up all night looking through her amazing collection of children's books, igniting a passion that I have continued to develop over the years, except that the books I collect are more representative of the diversity found in my global setting.

Teaching Experiment 2: The Study of Funds of Knowledge in Local Latinx Communities

Returning from my sabbatical for the fall of 1995 with renewed energy, a new passion for children's literature, and a clearer understanding of the study of funds of knowledge in Arizona, I was determined to transform the required bilingual research and evaluation course that I was assigned into a collaborative research project on funds of knowledge in local Latinx communities. Funds of knowledge represents one variant of culturally responsive teaching that builds on the resources of the home to connect the two most important socializing forces in children's development. However, "seeing what's there" requires knowing what to look for and how to make sense of what we see, which is why visiting families that welcome us into their home requires preparation that begins with studying theories of literacy as a social practice. In conceptions of literacy as a social/cultural practice, socialization processes, not just educational processes, play a significant role in the construction of the meaning and uses of literacy (Street, 1995). Socialization is a process by which one becomes a competent member of a society through the transmission of social skills and knowledge (Ochs, 1988). Language socialization research examines how socialization processes produce competences to use language as less experienced members of a community, to participate in verbal interactions with older and/or more experienced members. Consequently, speech-mediated activities are key to the transmission of this knowledge. The sociocultural contexts in which interactions occur become part of the pragmatic and social meanings that are acquired by members of a given community, as they assume various communication and social roles (Ochs, 1988).

However, these culturally organized activities are complex, overlapping and intertwined. For example, literacy practices are almost always fully integrated into and constitute part of the very texture of wider practices that involve talk, interaction, values, and beliefs. In their study of a working-class community in Great Britain, Barton and Hamilton (1998) make transparent the diversity of literacies that are rooted in everyday experiences and serve everyday purposes through which people make sense of their lives. Because of their lower social value, vernacular or local literacies (in contrast to official, institutional, or colonial literacies such as essay writing) often go unrecognized in dominant discourses about literacies.

Barton and Hamilton (1998) identify six domains of day-to-day life in which literacy is central:

1. Organizing life, e.g., literacy associated with paying bills, keeping calendars and appointment books.
2. Personal communication, e.g., writing cards and letters to loved ones.
3. Private leisure, e.g., reading books and magazines, writing poetry to relax.
4. Documenting life, e.g., maintaining records of one's life: birth certificates, school reports, old address books, party souvenirs.
5. Sense making, i.e., literacy related to researching topics of interest or need, e.g., health, legal, employment, parenting.
6. Social participation, e.g., literacy associated with participation in groups and social clubs.

Other scholars emphasize that the significance of literacy in children's socialization lies in its relation to the transmission of morals, discipline, and social values (Graff, in Ochs, 1988).

In another line of inquiry, a multi-disciplinary team of scholars affiliated with the Center for Puerto Rican Studies has studied language use in East Harlem since the late 1970s. Zentella (1997) and Pedraza (1987), sociolinguists affiliated with El Centro, interpret the bilingual and multidialectal code switching among members of this community to be an expression of their different identities and social roles (e.g., gender). Pedraza explains that a person's migratory history is the most critical factor influencing language behavior. Zentella (1997) agrees and argues for the need to understand the conditions that give rise to language variation, such as how it is influenced and shaped by the larger political, socioeconomic, and cultural forces (the social context), including the specific dialects employed. Zentella's two-pronged longitudinal study of language learning and use, first among twenty households and subsequently including five households that branched out from these, found that "dense and multiplex" social networks (many kinship networks) in which households are embedded played a role in the socialization of younger members of the community. Moreover, changes in the language and literacy practices of the community are attributed to changes in the social networks with which younger members are affiliated. Zentella (1997) also found that books in the home were for children and "the most consistent daily reading by adults was provided by television" (p. 215). She also found that technology, generally, was a major source of print in the households she studied.

As course instructor, I guided and assisted in the research process by introducing and explaining these key ideas, drawing on relevant academic readings, specifically grounded in theories of funds of knowledge, social networks, and literacy as a social practice. I also helped to scaffold how to conduct home observations and discussions. Teacher-researchers organized themselves into teams of no fewer than two members and preferably no larger than three, and I eventually joined seven of those teams in their home visits. The teacher-researchers frequently met to prepare for or debrief their experience, usually at a local restaurant soon after their visit, in the homes of colleagues, or my office.

The mid-1990s brought us into the homes of mostly first- and second-generation Puerto Rican migrants, and a few families from the Dominican Republic and Mexico as the "Latinization" of New York City was well underway. Families opened their hearts and homes to two to three Puerto Rican/Latinx educators who came to learn from them about how families lived culturally to survive in a large metropolis, focused on the role literacy played in the household's activities.

What we found surprised us every time: there are powerful literacy practices in English, Spanish, or a combination of the two, that are embedded in the daily activities of low-income Puerto Rican/Latinx households, and although some replicate the basic forms of literacy promoted in the school curriculum, many engage in literacy to address medical, economic, and spiritual/emotional needs. However, although our primary purpose was to understand literacy practices that reside in Latinx communities, our work was also guided by the belief that teachers need to understand the socio-historic political realities beyond the school that constrain much of what happens in the classroom.

Thus, fieldwork methods central to our collaborative research brought all of us out of our institutional settings to learn about and understand local homes and communities where teachers labor and students live. Even though I supervise early field experiences in these same communities, workload and other responsibilities leave little time to examine how changing demographics affect children's lives as well as the curriculum and the learning-teaching process. In effect, focused ethnographic fieldwork in local communities also serves as a form of professional development for classroom teachers as much as for faculty in schools of education.

This second "experiment" more than doubled the workload for one course with a heavy course load, but a commitment to community drives the never-ending quest to improve what we do as educators. As a faculty member with limited financial resources, I managed to do what I had to do in much the same way that families mine their social network to survive: we exchanged favors to meet mutual needs. Social scientists of the Center for Puerto Rican Studies of the City University of New York served as guest speakers, elaborating on sociological, economic, and sociocultural perspectives that shed light on the complex and sophisticated theoretical frameworks that shaped this research project. An unexpected opportunity to supervise a post-doctoral appointment sponsored by the Educational Testing Service (ETS) and the interest of graduate and doctoral students who responded to my call for assistance provided much needed assistance in preparing for conversations (not interviews) with caregivers in the home.

However, I found it surprising that Latinx teachers/graduate students had limited, if any, knowledge of the contributions Puerto Rican/Latinx scholars are making to a holistic understanding of the educational problems we confront, suggesting that studies that inform our work as educators remain hidden, both in the academy and in an educational system that may benefit from this scholarship. Clearly, without these sources of support, this experimental study would not have been possible; neither would it have been possible without the most important asset we brought—we were Latinx people who spoke Spanish, some with greater fluency than others. This bilingualism and biliteracy were distributed in the group; a collective and individual fund of knowledge that guided the phrasing of questions, and that facilitated the give and take of open-ended conversations. In effect, our biliteracy was also a critical factor in building *confianza*, or trusting relationships, that are prerequisites to gaining access to what we wanted to understand: literacy practices that might have otherwise gone unnoticed. In this study, and in all our collaborative activities (including teaching), the process for constructing new knowledge is social and dependent on the relationships we develop with each other, and with the participating caregivers and children we seek to learn from.

Many of the literacy practices that we documented during our home visits related to making sense of lived experience, and addressed a range of needs that included understanding (1) health and nutrition, (2) legal issues affecting household members, (3) the upbringing of children, (4) one's identity and the identities of those who are new to our community, and (5) the need for spiritual comfort and guidance. Research to learn about health concerns that affect family and friends usually begins with literature that is available in the hospital or clinic waiting room and that is relevant to the lives of families, but extends outward and involves conversations with experts (those with lived experience and those with formal knowledge of the subject) and interaction with other symbolic media, e.g., informational videos. In effect, literacy as a sense-making practice is an ongoing quest to understand, through multiple symbolic media or multiple literacies, information motivated by a need to assist or comfort loved ones, another way in which literacy is tied to relationships. These uses of literacy are not likely to be visible through questions such as, "What kinds of things do you read?"

Teacher-researchers who have visited the homes of Latinx families describe the range of funds of knowledge that are embedded in the day-to-day existence of modest income homes. The validation of community knowledge resulting from these visits transforms the relationship among students, families, and teachers, and the expectations teachers hold for students. Thus this collaborative inquiry approach to the study of funds of knowledge proves powerful for bridging home–school uses of language and literacy and strengthening the relationship between the school and the home.

The study of community funds of knowledge is also a powerful form of teacher development, particularly in large urban centers where even teachers with experience are challenged to address the constantly changing diversity of their student population and the many issues associated with poverty that affect schooling. Darling-Hammond (1998) has asserted that "What teachers know and can do is one of the most important influences on what students learn" (p. 6), especially students from low-income communities who are more dependent on schools than their more privileged counterparts to develop mainstream social and cultural capital needed to be successful in school. As Cochran-Smith (1995, p. 504) concludes, teachers must come to know the schools and communities in which they teach because

> teaching occurs within a particular historical and social moment and is embedded within nested layers of context, including the social and academic structures of the classroom; the history and norms of teaching and learning at the school; and the attitudes, values and beliefs, and language uses of the community and its web of historical, political, and social relationships to the school.

Therefore, curriculum construction and pedagogy must be variable if it is to be locally appropriate and culturally sensitive.

Through this retrospective analysis I have come to understand that we have the responsibility to make these lived experiences public, because those who sponsor and support public education have a right to know that the sources of educational problems reported in the press are often the result of hastily and politically motivated policy by high-level management, which school administrators and educators are obligated to follow. I have also gained greater appreciation for the hardworking classroom teachers who give themselves to challenging work not simply to meet course requirements, but as a form of service to community in the interest of the children they serve. What follows are a few insightful comments that they have shared locally and at international conferences:

> The knowledge I obtained from my project did not come from the things I expected; it came from the surprises, the unexpected. I thought I knew where my students come from. I thought I knew what their experiences were like. I've often said, "I know my students' stories because I've been there." Well I was wrong. I have a lot to learn. Times have changed and conditions for many of these children are worse than expected. Children live in fear of what could happen to them and their families.
>
> The family lives in a brick, two-story structure. Although the structure was built to house two families, it has been converted; it has been converted into a four-family dwelling, resulting in very small, cramped quarters.
>
> I learned from the family about love, despair, hope, survival, and happiness. Mrs. Perez is a fighter, a woman of tremendous courage. Because her husband's health is rapidly failing, she is singlehandedly holding the family together. She goes to school, looks for work, does volunteer work and takes care of the home and the family. Mrs. Perez is a survivor, a highly intelligent woman who does not give up.
>
> Mr. M. created this newspaper in Brazil and continued its development in the United States. Its publication is on an international level on a monthly basis. Although the father is the main editor, the daughter contributes the social events. Mrs. M. also takes part in the production and editing of the family newspaper.

As I have come to understand, engaging in collaborative research in local communities where children of the working poor live and attend school is a form of embodied learning, a construct I first encountered in Canadian scholarship and one that Dr. Fred Erickson captures when he described our work in the Middle School as "work done with the heart, the mind and the body." Embodied learning might include bearing witness to small moments in the lives of families to observe their social worlds and experience the sights, sounds, and smells of the objects and artifacts of the physical space, and the limitations imposed by scarce financial resources or impoverished living conditions. Telling or explaining that where you live affects how you experience life and the quality of the educational experiences and services you receive is far less effective than experiencing what these words mean to real people. Consequently, we found that academic readings made more sense after our embodied experiences in the home, where we witnessed first-hand the resourcefulness of families struggling to survive under challenging conditions.

Both the middle school collaboration and the funds of knowledge project proved to be very powerful approaches for connecting teacher-researchers to different scholarly communities where teacher-researchers gain well-deserved recognition for insights and contributions they are making to the knowledge base on teaching in low-income, working-class communities (see, e.g., Brookline Teacher Researcher Seminar, 2003). It was exhausting and gratifying work that remains memorable and fresh all these years. However, what I did not remember when I embarked upon these two small-scale collaborative experiments is that school–university collaborations to improve schooling experiences for "language minority" learners date back to the experimental instructional approaches that resulted from the Bilingual Education Act of 1968. Through their collaboration, Au and Jordan (1981) developed an alternative way to teach reading comprehension by combining features of learning in school with those of learning at home. It was similar to the approach Ashton-Warner introduced in New Zealand and that the federally funded Funds of Knowledge approach accomplished through teacher study groups that developed instructional applications from the findings from the household studies. Moreover, the Kamehameha Early Education Program (Project Keep) "developed from a 15-year continuous research and development program for improving the cognitive and educational development of at-risk ethnic minority children in Hawaii (Au & Jordan, 1981; Tharp & Gallimore, 1988). As Tharp and Gallimore (1988) explain, the program was interdisciplinary and multi-methodological, based firmly on inquiry and dedicated simultaneously to producing educational success according to strict evaluation. These different initiatives also demonstrate significant improvement on standardized reading test, without resorting to "test prep" as a ubiquitous and costly practice in under-resourced urban schools, reducing the curriculum to reading, mathematics, and test prep.

Part Three

Teaching to Learn in the Community

Teaching to Learn in a Changing Policy Context

This chapter focuses on my experiences as a teaching educator in the last three years before retirement, when I had already earned the distinction of full professor and had devoted many years to clinical practice in schools in transnational communities that serve the children of the poor. During those final years as full-time faculty, I came to a new understanding of what Britzman (2003) means when she says that experience also has its limitations, having to learn to teach anew in a policy context that changed *whom* we taught and *what* we taught. Those we taught were accomplished adults recruited through national searches to teach in low-scoring schools in high poverty communities in New York City, with incentives from the federal government through the No Child Left Behind Act (NCLB) of 2002. What we taught was also linked to NCLB funding for preparing pre- and in-service teachers in an approach to early reading instruction, as mentioned in Chapter 1, referred to as Reading First. "Reading First" was a new name for a familiar approach to reading instruction that emphasizes the relationship between the print–sound code. What is new (and concerning) is that this approach to early reading instruction was introduced as an approach that will narrow the achievement gap between middle income and high poverty schools.

As the fall 2008 semester was about to begin, faculty specializing in literacy was pressed to collaborate on common assignments and assessments for a new, first semester developmental reading course that reflected the influence of federal funding on teacher preparation in New York State. We were asked to work on these tasks with the urgency that meeting new state certification requirements demanded, without jeopardizing our stellar reputation as a service one institution. New certification requirements were issued by the state educational agency, with recommendations from professional organizations that inform the preparation of teachers in the core content of reading and English Language Arts. The NCLB, which made possible experimentation with alternative approaches to literacy instruction in two languages to children who, like me, came from homes where languages other than English were spoken, now sponsored a singular approach to early reading instruction in English and promoted curriculum standardization in teacher preparation.

Guided by the new course description, I prepared my fall 2008 course syllabus to include the topic of child development, selecting accessible readings that addressed how the experience of poverty shapes the development of children who live in segregated, low-income communities. Garcia Coll and Szalacha (1996) provide what I consider to be a clear explanation of how poverty, racism, and discrimination result in developmental risks. They also bring to light how children are resilient and that these experiences also lead to the development of assets or strengths when there are sources of emotional support in their homes and communities, including teachers and other members of school staff. What the various readings I reviewed make very clear is that the conditions under which children develop in homes where family income falls far below the poverty level are very different from the white, middle-class norm of development that drives mainstream teacher preparation (Weisner, 2002). These differences are commonly neglected when comparisons of children's school progress and development are made. It concerned me that little attention was given to these differences in clinical practice (or methods) courses, in a teacher education program where the required child development course was situated in the department of educational foundations. Moreover, for as long as I can remember, Piaget's theory of child development remained the dominant perspective.

In truth, the content requirements of clinical practice (or methods) courses offered in the department of curriculum and teaching leave little time for thoughtful exploration of these issues, which include how isolation and prejudice often rob even successful students of their self-confidence and self-worth, and the influence of these experiences on children's literacy development in and for school purposes. However, a diverse group of scholars agree that instruction may play an important role in mitigating the negative influence of poverty on school learning (Beck & McKeown, 2001; Diaz, Moll & Mehan, 1986; Moll, 1988; Tikunoff, 1985).

I confirmed these findings in a small-scale, multi-year collaborative project (more like a service project), which I described in Chapter 4. Sixth-graders were exposed to an inquiry-oriented, writing intensive approach to reading and writing development, in one of the lowest scoring middle schools, in one of the poorest communities in the city. The positive impact that this instructional experiment had on the socioemotional and intellectual development of children who doubted their ability to engage in what I described as "college work" was remarkable. Although we did not set out with the singular focus on improving scores on standardized tests in reading and writing, that is precisely what happened. Scholarship that I trace to the 1970s suggests that these outcomes reflect the power of strong, positive relationships with adults who believe in children's ability to learn in combination with an instructional approach that is challenging and that elevates the status of children who are unaccustomed to feeling special in school. Ours was a supportive learning community (some sixth graders described it as a "family") that extended beyond the walls of the classroom, guided by adults who cared deeply about the whole child. Although punitive grade retention policies left scars, sixth graders as old as fourteen years of age overcame insecurities formed through experiences that began in their first year of schooling, and that robbed them of their self-esteem and confidence in their capacity to learn. This experience also demonstrated that there are different paths to attaining valued goals, and that we must be open to exploring these different and multiple possibilities when we work in the interest of the children, not of prescribed programs.

Thus, as the fall 2008 semester was about to begin, I could not help thinking about the policy context that shaped a professional journey, which began in 1969 as a result of a social policy that addressed the educational needs of local communities, in locally appropriate ways; and that for more than a decade encouraged experimentation with alternative instructional approaches for minoritized populations. This comparative perspective made me conscious of the need to pay greater attention to the influence of policy on work that is singularly focused on "practice," a topic I will return to in Chapter 6. As I have come to understand through this writing, each of these two policy contexts offered an alternative response to the experience of difference.

Alternative Responses to the Experience of Difference

In Chapters 3 and 4 I described how, in the 1960s, the federal government assumed an unprecedented role in formulating social policy to address the needs of U.S. citizens who reside in low-income communities, and are denied access to instruction in a language children and youth are able to understand. The Elementary and Secondary Education of 1968 (the same law that gave us the No Child Left Behind Act) and related legislative initiatives encouraged experimentation with special alternative instructional approaches, including bilingual instruction. However, novel experiments also incorporated traditional teaching practices, as is found in early reading instruction that combines attention to the print–sound code with the language experience approach to reading instruction.

The federal government also sponsored an ambitious research agenda, which has generated foundational thinking that informs reading and writing development and instruction. Still relevant are studies that captured the experience of learning at home and in school by children and families who live in low-income communities. For example, Heath's (1983) ethnographic research exposed how children across the racial divide and from working-class families were socialized to use language differently, at home and in school, in two racially diverse working-class communities in the Carolinas. The second part of this study engaged the ethnographer with local teachers to connect the home and the school, for the wellbeing of children.

Scholarship also documents the emergence of biliteracy before formal schooling, revealing how the innate curiosity of young children enables them to construct understandings of reading and writing in two languages without formal instruction (Edelsky, 1983; Hudelson, 1984; Teale & Sulzby, 1986). A similar process occurs when adults read aloud "big books" to children, following the line of print with a ruler or a pointer. Research also demonstrates the benefits of instruction that capitalizes on the knowledge and resources of local communities, including valuing its bilingualism as a social and intellectual asset, in a hemisphere where Spanish is as much a public language as is English. However, most affecting is research that reveals that positive relations with teachers in the classroom and between home and school appear to be less common for low-income and racial minority children than for higher income, Caucasian students (McDermott, 1977b; Hamre & Pianta, 2005). McDermott's conclusions merit attention: "Teaching and learning involves more than the curriculum, a style or a way of talking. Most of all it involves an achievement of mutual trust and accountability in terms of which pupils and teachers can open themselves to each other, care about each other and learn from each other" (1977b, in Panofsky, 2003, p. 427). Panofsky (2003) builds on McDermott's seminal study in New York City, and concludes: "The dynamic of social relations has been shown to be central in the experience of failure for many low-income students" (p. 411). However, Panofsky attributes these differential experiences to larger conflicts in society, pointing out that teachers need to be prepared to understand a dynamic that should be a major focus of teacher preparation. Understandings generated from timeless, seminal research should inform clinical practice courses that are designed to prepare teachers to teach in high poverty communities.

When I entered the department of curriculum and teaching in 1988, my immediate supervisors in curriculum and teaching and educational foundations recognized the value and relevance of this scholarship, and organized several faculty development sessions on multiculturalism, bilingualism, and language variation in my first years as "new" faculty, and invited me to share my experiences and understandings as a student and as a teacher educator. This early research remains vital and offers alternative ways to understand and respond to the experience of "difference" and "marginalization" associated with social economic inequalities that affects the great majority of U.S. citizens who live in communities where English and Spanish intermingle. This is the body of research that has informed my practice since I assumed a full-time faculty position such that now it forms part of my embodied knowing—knowledge that is integrated in my body and that shapes my stance as an educator. These are the uncommon perspectives that I brought to the literacy courses I taught, and that shaped my practice in the fall of 2008. This body of research is in sharp contrast to the body of research that informs mainstream teacher education, and that is likely to be familiar to teacher candidates. Figure 5.1 details how demographic factors affecting people living in poverty become institutionalized in school policy as pathologizing structures that perpetuate inequality.

However, as a new decade began in 1980, Chester Finn, the Assistant Secretary of Education in the newly elected administration, proclaimed a new vision: "The sixties and the seventies ended for American education, both literally and philosophically . . . instead of focusing single-mindedly on equality of opportunity, we also look for quality and for learning gaps to narrow" (Finn, 2004). A singular focus on narrowing the achievement gap by holding schools accountable for yearly progress has led to the use of testing not simply as a measure of outcomes, but as curriculum itself, reducing the school curriculum in low-income communities to basic reading, mathematics, and testing. This is a new version of the "pedagogy of the poor" that Haberman (1991) describes, which I elaborated on in Chapter 4. I know from experience of supervising clinical practice in low-income communities, that this pedagogy is pervasive in local public schools. The changes that Finn announced also halted the practice of investing in individuals with a range of talents and abilities, who in diversifying the teaching workforce also normalize difference and the social and intellectual benefits that may come from diversity, more so in the nation's only global city, as Milem (2005) explains. I benefitted from those investments, and service to others, as a life project.

- Children five to six years of age are identified (stigmatized) as being at-risk of school failure based on demographic characteristics and the display of behavioral, attention, academic, social problems reported by their kindergarten teachers (Hamre & Pianta, 2005).
- Students from ethnic/racial minorities tend to do poorer on measured achievement in reading and language arts than students from mainstream backgrounds throughout the elementary school years and end up, on average, about four years behind in secondary school (National Research Council study; Snow, Burns & Griffin, 1998).
- Positive relations with teachers in the classroom and between home and school appear to be less common for low-income and racial minority children than for higher income, Caucasian students (Entwisle & Alexander, 1993). Early racial and income differences in relatedness may contribute to disparities in achievement (Pianta, Rimm-Kaufman & Cox, 1999).
- Schools in economically depressed communities make more contacts with families about the problems and difficulties that their children are having, unless they work at developing balanced partnership programs that include contact about positive accomplishments of students (Epstein, 1995).
- Although low-income students in grades two and three achieve as well as children in the normative population on subtests of learning to read, students' scores start to decelerate around grade four, when reading becomes a tool for learning. Teachers of disadvantaged children report this "fourth grade slump" (Chall & Jacobs, 2003).
- Out of seventy-nine full days of observation, low SES classrooms spend a mean of 1.9 percent of time on informational books. If we assume that books are a key resource for knowledge and vocabulary, informational texts may provide a central source for developing areas of expertise for children from disadvantaged communities who have limited access to resources (Neuman, 2001).
- Although reading aloud to children is a common practice in schools in low-income communities, not all read-aloud practices promote language and literacy development (Beck & McKeown, 2001).
- Most classroom writing is in response to tests or homework assignments with the teacher as the primary audience and evaluator. Writing is rarely needed as a broad tool of communication—to convey opinions and ideas or to analyze and explore the world (Diaz, Moll & Mehan, 1986).

Figure 5.1 Social Inequalities in Learning to Read and Write

By 2008, schools and districts with increasingly high numbers of children on "free lunch" (an indicator of poverty) had been implementing "Reading First" for several years, as cash-strapped state and local educational agencies submitted proposals the minute funds were made available. Because of the close working relationship between the City University system and the Department of Education, in 2005 the leadership of our teacher education programs responded to the call to prepare thousands of accomplished adults and elite college graduates (also referred to as "the best and the brightest") as a response to serious teacher shortages, including in schools where Reading First was now well established. However, the state's largest school district with high levels of poverty also has high numbers of English language learners from every corner of the world, the great majority from Spanish-speaking homes and communities, and a smaller, but increasing, percentage of children who speak Chinese at home, and who reside in transnational communities with a large concentration of Chinese-speakers. I feared that initial reading instruction that is narrowly focused on "phonemic awareness" tasks, which require young children to recognize the discrete sounds (phonemes) that comprise a word, augments the challenge of learning to read in English, even by those who have lived in the United States all of their lives. English is an alphabetic language. An alphabet is a writing system based on the phoneme. Alphabetic writing is unnatural because it splits sounds in speech in a way they don't normally split. The English alphabet code is complex because it lacks one-to-one correspondence between each sound in the language and the symbol that represents it, as Spanish does. Consequently, it is easier for English learners from homes where Spanish is the language of family life to learn to read in Spanish. Equally concerning is that these policies fail to grasp or wilfully refuse to acknowledge the significance of sociocultural and socioemotional influences on school learning.

It bears repeating: American children shaped by the experience of marginalization associated with social and economic inequalities enter school with both developmental risks (and assets that remain invisible) that affect their relationship with peers and adults and their engagement with instructional content, including standardized tests. During clinical supervision in local schools, I witnessed, first-hand, how young children in grades one and two responded to a demanding new test culture. It literally made them sick to their stomach, as even young children were aware of how these tests affected their experiences in school. On other occasions, I observed the even more intimidating experience of being subjected to individually administered, early reading assessments twice yearly, an experience that robs young children of precious instructional time in the critical first years of schooling. This untenable situation led parents to organize massive protests against the new test culture, which they describe as a form of child abuse. State-wide protests by coalitions of concerned parents and educators that bridged class differences eventually led to a change in policy in the early grades. These are among the issues that literacy faculty confronted as the fall 2008 semester got underway. In truth, there is simply too much testing in this country, more so than in any other major industrialized nation in the world where testing is used selectively to assess preparation for significant transitions in schooling.

One of the challenges that I confronted was that the accomplished adults who were being recruited by the Department of Education through a national search knew little about the realities they were likely to encounter in New York City schools, beginning with the physical size and age of schools and their locations in low-income communities. The ten hours of classroom observation that the teacher certification unit required in a first course on "developmental reading" (five hours in grades one to three; and five in grades four to six) offered but a brief glimpse into classroom instruction in the nation's largest school system, with over 1,000 elementary schools and programs. Consequently, it was a serious responsibility to prepare novices to teach the first of two required "literacy methods" courses, the most important core content area of the childhood education curriculum, to children who need teachers who know *how* to teach them or who, at the very least, know how to *relate* to the children that attend local public schools. If they are good observers and good listeners, the children they are expected to teach may even assist in their development as teachers.

Even more concerning is that reading was and is still narrowly defined as a collection of basic skills that once mastered enables the reading and comprehension of all manner of written texts. Cultural critic E.D. Hirsch (1988) critiques this false assumption in an aptly titled article, "They can read, but they can't understand," to emphasize the importance of knowledge in reading comprehension for adults as much as for children. As a specialist in early reading instruction, Susan Neuman (2001) also calls attention to the role of knowledge in early literacy.

I also found it concerning that writing was initially omitted from the preliminary course syllabus, overlooking the mutually supportive relationship between reading and writing in developmental reading. At that time, I was strongly influenced by the perspective and practice that Wells and Chang (1990) articulated: "it is in the activity of writing that the nature of literacy is most readily grasped, and the potential of language for empowering thinking most fully experienced" (p. 134). Although no one disputes that reading alphabetic languages involves deciphering the print–sound code, reading (or literacy) continues to evolve and change in a technologically advanced, knowledgeable society.

In the early grades I prefer to develop positive emotional connections to reading (and writing), emphasizing that reading has magical powers. It can transport us to imaginary worlds and take us to faraway places, even a trip to the moon, as the main character conveys in Ezra Jack Keats' (1981) story, *Regards to the Man in the Moon*. Holdaway (1979) demonstrated the benefits of listening to stories read aloud, or what he referred to as the shared book experience, which some children enjoy at home and others enjoy in school. While reading aloud, the teacher is also modeling fluent reading, one of the five core skills emphasized in Reading First. Children who are English learners are more likely to demonstrate fluent reading when they engage in "pretend" reading than when they are required to combine decoding and fluent reading as they focus on the line of print. It is no exaggeration to say that adults learning to teach developmental reading are often reluctant to read aloud in class, in part because they find this seemingly simple task challenging. Frank Smith (1978) explains that, over time, through the shared book experience, children also develop fundamental insights about print—that print is meaningful and that print is language. Children may also begin to take notice that the language of books is different from spoken language. As Smith concludes, it may be more important to read with children because, even when they are dependent on the expert reader initially, over time they develop competence and confidence to want to manage on their own. Even so, it is the responsibility of the teacher to assist in these understandings and development. Clearly, teachers will need to be on the alert for evidence that these changes are taking place. Figure 5.2 provides an overview of some fundamental understandings that new teachers should develop in organizing responsive learning environments in high poverty schools.

In the rush to complete our assigned tasks of collaborating on common assignments and assessments, there was no time to partake in these conversations with professional colleagues who would be teaching the new developmental reading course in the fall of 2008. I felt I had a spiritual "ally" in Jeanne Chall, a major (albeit controversial) authority on "developmental reading," a term she coined for a stage theory of reading that has been discredited by sociocultural scholars who study language and literacy development in low-income, working-class communities (e.g., Heath, 1983; Dyson, 1993). Chall subsequently concluded that low-income children in grades two and three achieve as well as children in the normative population. However, their performance on standardized tests starts to decelerate around grade four, commonly referred to as the "fourth-grade slump" (Chall & Jacobs, 2003). Chall and Jacobs attribute

Literacy is not just a matter of skills or cognitive strategies; it is also a matter of will or feelings and emotions.

Winograd & Paris, 1988

Literacy is far more than a skill. It requires large amounts of specific information.

Hirsch, 1988, p. 2

Literacy development begins long before children start formal instruction. Children use legitimate reading and writing behaviors in the informal setting of the home and community.

Teale & Sulzby, 1986

Teaching and learning depend fundamentally on the quality of the relationship between teachers and students.

McDonald, Kazemi & Schneider Kavanagh, 2013; McDermott, 1977b

Instruction plays an important role in extending the range of experiences students have with literacy (Moll, 1988). However instruction is only useful when it moves ahead of development.

Vygotsky in Daniels, 2007

Reading aloud to children encourages growth in language and literacy when it provides experiences with decontextualized language, requiring children to make sense of ideas that are beyond the here and now, as Text Talk does.

Beck & McKeown, 2001

Respond to the diversity of learners with an appropriately diverse range of approaches.

Davydov in Daniels, 2007, p. 316

To teach well the teacher must connect the subject matter to the needs, desires, interests, and intellectual development, etc of the students within the physical, social, political context that the teachers and students find themselves.
Garrison & Neiman, 2003, p. 29. Garrison and Neiman paraphrase Dewey, 1916

There is no simple answer to how to work with children in the classroom. It is a matter of being present as a whole person with your own thoughts and feelings, and of accepting children as whole people, with their own thoughts and feelings … and working very hard to find out what those thoughts and feelings are.

Duckworth, 1986

Figure 5.2 Understandings Needed to Teach Developmental Reading in Poor Communities

the "slump" to dramatic changes in the literacy demands of the fourth-grade curriculum, and argue that children need earlier exposure to reading informational books.

Bridging Differences

With heightened consciousness of the shifting emphasis in the curriculum at grade four, and the challenges I confronted, I integrated the two major themes of learning to read and reading to learn in the syllabus, and in practice gave priority to "reading and writing" to learn. It made sense to combine reading and writing to learn within the study of information picture books written in the more engaging narrative structure, rather than the more complex structure of expository prose. For these many reasons, I find truth in the claims of respected scholars (Luke, 2004; Ovando, 2004; Weiner, 2007): federal and state regulations governing the preparation of teachers in a critical area of the curriculum are ideologically driven.

I am also mindful that the syllabus is a legal document that should maintain a level of consistency across multiple sections of the same course, including the professional language we use to represent the content of instruction, even if our interpretations of this language differ. I exercised my academic freedoms in organizing learning experiences and selecting course materials that I believed merited attention, some of which I posted on blackboard (bb), our institutional online website for the course, for easy access, as I did with informative materials on Reading First developed by Armbruster and Armstrong for the Center for Improvement of Early Reading Achievement. This is a publication everyone agreed offered a clear explanation of the "building blocks for teaching children to read."

As social beings with the capacity for collective and mediated agency, we exert the power that resides in relationships, not individuals, to push back against forces that disrupt our work as educators, and doing so also changes us. I embraced the challenges that this new situation presented, sustaining my focus on what mattered: I transformed marginality into a site of resistance, as bell hooks (1994) theorizes, in the interest of the children we serve through the teachers we prepare. However. I did so mindful of my responsibilities to the adults I am preparing to teach.

It is noteworthy that, in the midst of these changes, the New York City Department of Education was also undergoing major restructuring, now officially under mayoral control during the administration of Michael Bloomberg, with over one million school children, an increasing number living in temporary shelters or hotels. Local reforms incorporated key features of NCLB by holding schools accountable for the academic achievement of all students and assuring that the teaching and paraprofessional staff was "highly qualified," most likely based on scores on professional exams and grade point averages. The press for accountability through students' performance on standardized tests (the new mantra) may also explain the emphasis on core skills of Reading First that are tested on standardized tests.

Almost simultaneously, in 2002, the new Deputy Chancellor for Instruction under Chancellor Joel Klein, Carmen Farina, introduced a new literature-based Balanced Literacy approach to reading and writing instruction. The overview that the New York City Department of Education (NYC DOE) posted on their website in 2002 presented a set of guidelines that outlined the major reading and writing activities that should receive attention on a daily basis, including reading aloud to children, reading with children, and reading independently. Thus, the official DoED approach, which eventually merged with the "Reading and Writing Workshop" instructional model developed by Lucy Calkins, created an opening to work for the goals that I value.

What appears to be new in the Reading and Writing Workshop model is that a ninety-minute block of time is devoted to reading and writing instruction, where children play active roles in the process, often spending lengthy stretches of time working independently. In my professional opinion, I do not think it appropriate to allow children who need access to instructional support to spend long stretches of time on independent activities. This may explain why the Balanced Literacy approach may be more popular in the more affluent districts. However, the focal activity in this approach is the teacher-guided, interactive read aloud that combines evidence-based comprehension with mini-lessons focused on core skills and strategies (e.g., phonics, comprehension) identified through grade level standards that stretch over five days of instruction. The Interactive Read Aloud is considered a high utility core practice and identified as a "best practice" for bilingual and English Learners because it is associated with a sustained pattern of improvement on standardized tests of reading (Development & Dissemination Project, 1999). Beck and McKeown (2001) developed an adaptation of the Interactive Read Aloud referenced as "Text Talk" to assist teachers in guiding young children who are English Learners to benefit from the read aloud experience that focuses on the literary language of text. Strategies emphasize building meaning from text through open-ended questions, focused discussion at appropriate junctures, and explicit attention to vocabulary (see Figure 5.3). According to the researchers, the approach is designed to reduce the influence of illustrations, background/vocabulary knowledge that interfere with constructing textually appropriate meaning (Beck & McKeown, 2001). Although

---

Text

- Select texts that give children ideas to ponder and explain.
- Text is organized as a narrative of connected events or as series of disconnected situations.
- The linguistic content is primary.
- Contains rare or unusual words, which are focused on during presentation.

Initial Questions

- Open questions should prompt student talk.
  - "What do you notice on the front cover?"
  - "What clues do the author and illustrator give us?

Follow Up Questions
Follow up on responses to initial questions to elicit meaningful responses rather than asking more questions.

- Build on response to open questions, eliciting elaboration, and explanation.
- Repeat and rephrase what student was saying to encourage elaboration.
- Follow up with a generic probe, "What do you mean by that?"
- Reread a portion of the text and repeat the initial question.

Pictures/Illustrations
Remind children to listen to the words of the story.
Wait to show pictures when . . .

- Pictures mirror the linguistic content of the text.
- The content of pictures conflicts with the message of text.

Background Knowledge
Help children use their background knowledge appropriately to understand stories.

Vocabulary
Call attention to how a word (e.g., rare, multiple meanings) is used in context and elaborate on its meaning.

Figure 5.3 Text Talk as a Tool to Enhance Children's Language Development

---

Text Talk is intended to support children's understanding of literary language (for example, the metaphors and similes that appear in the picture book, *Nina Bonita* (Machado, [1995] 2001)) as well as decontextualized language, I have explored broader uses, as I illustrate in my preview lesson on Rachel.

The teaching guide that Lucy Calkins developed for the Reading and Writing Workshop also includes scripted lessons that are correlated to read aloud texts, sequenced, and paced for each grade. Although these scripts may have been intended to support the professional development of teachers who are new to the program, I had a surreal experience one day as I walked through the corridors of a school and I heard the same script being recited, almost in unison, by different teachers, in their own classrooms. In that moment I came face to face with a level of standardization that was unimaginable to me at the turn of the twenty-first century. Knowing of the inclusion of scripts in Calkins Reading and Writing Workshop motivated me to develop my own teaching scripts. One, I wanted to demystify this practice and two, I wanted to make clear that professionals are capable of writing their own scripts, to benefit from thinking about and writing down how they want to introduce a book. I anticipated that, after having the experience of developing their own scripts, course participants would be less inclined to have someone else put words into their mouth.

What I do like about the mandated reading program is that the literature-based balanced literacy approach does not neglect the "core skills" of learning to read. Rather, it provides a meaningful context for the teaching of these core skills. I consider that this contextual support is likely to assist English learners to understand and apply these core skills to other readings. Also, second career teaching aspirants are expected to understand and teach lessons on phonics, fluency, vocabulary (which are mostly subsumed under word study), and reading comprehension, always connected to the storyline of the picture book that is the focus of the Interactive Read Aloud. Teach for America (TfA) developed an approach to literacy that builds on New York City's mandated balanced literacy program, with their particular emphasis on the primacy of decoding skills, as is emphasized in the Reading First instructional program sponsored by NCLB. TfA has taken this approach globally through Teach for All; however, what I found concerning is that on one full page of research citations, not a single reference is made to the assets that children in poor communities bring to learning to read in school. Figure 5.4 presents a few examples.

A few excerpts from a full page of print:

Research conducted by the National Institute for Child Health and Development has found that more than 74 percent of children *who enter first grade at-risk of reading failure* will continue to struggle to read into adulthood. It is disturbing, but perhaps not surprising that the literacy skills of students in the under-resourced schools where we teach, often lag well behind those of children in wealthier areas.

Almost 70 percent of low-income fourth grade students cannot read at basic level.

Similarly, the National Assessment of Educational Progress surveys in 1998 found discrepancies in writing skills of students by socioeconomic status.

These poor reading outcomes no doubt reflect the accumulated effects of several risk factors including lack of access to literacy-stimulating preschool experiences and to excellent, coherent reading instruction in the early elementary grades.

Figure 5.4 Deficit-Oriented Views of Teach for America
Source: https://www.teachforamerica.org/life-in-the-corps/corps-member-training

In 2002, the DoED also allocated funds to ensure that each classroom had a well-stocked collection of picture books and trade books by best-selling authors, the heart of the new mandated "Balanced Literacy" approach to reading and writing instruction that is, in effect, a new variety of the whole language approach that emerged in the 1970s and 1980s, and that was very popular in low-income communities in areas with high concentrations of Spanish-speaking families. The two big differences that I recollect are that children learn to read and write in their primary language, for example English for some and Spanish for others, and that children in the sole language approach appear to engage in more teacher-directed activities than they do in the Reading and Writing Workshop.

Compared with dull workbooks and stories, written with a didactic intent focused on "reading skills," that are commonly found in under-resourced schools, enchanting picture books written in simple (and complex) lyrical prose that adults enjoy as much as children, convey to children who live in homes and communities below the poverty level that they are important. For this reason, for the past two decades I have grown a diverse collection of children's books on a wide-range of topics representative of geographic locations, written by award-winning authors from the United States, the Caribbean, Mesoamerica, and South

America, that make possible an interdisciplinary approach to reading and writing instruction. The great majority of books from my collection are not on the list that appears in the Teacher's Guide of the Reading and Writing Workshop (see Figure 5.5). I consider these stories to be far more representative of the heritages of the school population—including their origins, their interests, their concerns, and their substantive content—as many books that appear on lists of recommended books by professional organizations in social studies and science. I have discovered some books at international conferences sponsored by the International Board of Books for Youth (IBBY) where children's books are discussed and displayed (see Figure 5.6), and a few through the recommendations of colleagues based in the southwest and in California. I integrated "learning to read and write" and "reading and writing to learn" as the two major themes of "developmental reading," guided by the new common core standards and the LCI approach to contextualizing a work of art that facilitates textual comprehension through a range of media.

Ada, A.F. (2002). *I Love Saturdays y domingos*. New York: Atheneum Books for Young Readers.

Alba, J. (1994). *Calor: A Story of Warmth for All Ages* (English and Spanish Edition). OH: Aims Intl Books Corp.

Alire Saenz, B. (1998). *A Gift from Papa Diego*. El Paso, TX: Cinco Puntos Press.

Alonso, F. (1978). *El hombrecito vestido de gris* (The Little Man Dressed in Grey). Madrid: Alfaguara.

Alvarez, J. (2001). *How Tia Lola Came to Visit Stay*. New York: Yearling Books.

Ancona, G. (2003). *Murals: Walls that Sing*. Tarrytown, NY: Marshall Cavendish.

Andrews-Goebel, N. (2002). *The Pot that Juan Built*. New York: Lee & Low Books, Inc.

Baye, E. (1986). *Seis puntos apartes* (The Story of Braille). Barcelona, Spain: Aliorna, SA Editorial.

Brown, D. (1999). *Rare Treasure: Mary Anning and Her Remarkable Discovery*. New York: Houghton Mifflin Company.

Brown, M. (2005). *My Name is Gabriella*. Lanham: Cooper Square Publishing LLC.

Cameron, A. (1988). *El lugar mas bonito del mundo* (The Most Beautiful Place in the World). Mexico: Alfaguara.

Castaneda, O.S. (1995). *Abuela's Weave*. New York: Lee & Low Books.

Crandall, R. (2002). *Hands of the Maya*. New York: Henry Holt & Co.

Del Rosario, R. and I. Freire de Matos (1968). *ABC de Puerto Rico*. Sharon, CT: Troutman Press.

Dr. Seuss (1996). *My Many Colored Days.* New York: Alfred A. Knopf, Inc.

Ehrlich, A. (2008). *Rachel: The Story of Rachel Carson.* New York: Harcourt Children's Books.

Fleischman, P. (1997/2002). *Seedfolks.* New York: HarperCollins Publishers.

Henkes, K. (1991). *Chrysanthemum.* New York: HarperCollins.

Herrera, J.F. (2003). *Super Cilantro Girl.* New York: Children's Book Press.

Hesse, K. (1996). *The Music of Dolphins.* New York: Scholastic Press.

Jimenez, F. (2001). *Breaking Through: A Sequel to The Circuit.* New York: Houghton Mifflin Harcourt Children's Books.

Johnston, T. (2003). *Isabel's House of Butterflies.* San Francisco, CA: Sierra Book Club for Children.

Joseph, L. (2000). *The Color of My Words.* New York: HarperCollins Publishers.

Keats, E.J. (1960). *My Dog is Lost.* New York: Thomas Y. Crowell (now Viking).

Keister, D. (2001). *Fernando's Gift.* San Francisco, CA: Sierra Book Club for Children.

Kogan Ray, D. (1976/1977). *To Go Singing through the World: The Childhood of Pablo Neruda.* New York: Farrar, Straus and Giroux.

Lau-Carling, A. (2005). *Saw Dust Carpets.* Toronto, Ontario: Groundwood Books.

Lazaro, G. (2005). *Julia.* New York: Lectorum.

Leaf, M. (1936). *Ferdinand.* New York: Viking Press.

Lomas Garza, C. (1996). *In My Family/En mi familia.* San Francisco, CA: Children's Book Press.

Machado, A.M. (2002/2005). *From Another World.* Sao Paulo, Brazil: Editora Attic.

Mohr, N. (1979). *Felita.* New York: Dial Books.

Mora, P. (1997). *Tomas and the Library Lady.* New York: Alfred A. Knopf Inc.

Munoz Ryan, P. (2001). *Esperanza Rising.* New York: Scholastic Press.

Paola, T. de (2001). *Erandi's Braids.* New York: Puffin Books.

Perera, H. (1984). *Kike.* Madrid: Imprenta SM.

Rockwell, N. (1994). *Wilie was Different.* Stickbridge, MA: Bookshire House Publishers.

Shihab Nye, N. (1994). *Sitti's Secrets.* New York: Aladdin Paperback edition.

Trevino, E.B. (1989). *El guero: A True Adventure Story.* New York: Farrar Straus Giroux.

Velasquez, E. (2001). *Grandma's Records.* New York: Walker Publishing Co.

Young, E. (1997). *Voices of the Heart.* New York: Scholastic Press.

Figure 5.5 Children's Books for Elementary School Readers

The International Board on Books for Young People (IBBY) is a nonprofit organization that represents an international network of people from all over the world who are committed to bringing books and children together. IBBY's mission is: to promote international understanding through children's books; to give children everywhere the opportunity to have access to books with high literary and artistic standards; to encourage the publication and distribution of quality children's books, especially in developing countries; to provide support and training for those involved with children and children's literature; to stimulate research and scholarly works in the field of children's literature; to protect and uphold the Rights of the Child according to the UN Convention on the Rights of the Child.

IBBY was founded in Zurich, Switzerland, in 1953. Today, it is composed of seventy-five National Sections all over the world. It represents countries with well-developed book publishing and literacy programs, and other countries with only a few dedicated professionals who are doing pioneer work in children's book publishing and promotion.

The Children's Book Council is a not-for-profit association that encourages the use and enjoyment of books and related literacy materials for young people. Its members are publishers of trade books for children and producers of book-related materials for young people. CBC cooperates on reading development projects with several national associations including the National Council for Social Studies (NCSS) and the National Science Teachers Association (NSTA).

The National Council for the Social Studies (NCSS) is a professional, non-profit association for teachers and social studies educators at all levels from early childhood through college. It engages and supports teachers in strengthening and advocating social studies. The book review committee looks for books that emphasize human relations, represent a diversity of groups and are sensitive to a broad range of cultural experiences, present an original theme or a fresh slant on a traditional topic, are easily readable and of high literary quality, have a pleasing format, and, where appropriate, include illustrations that enrich the text. Each book is read by several reviewers, and included on the list by committee assent. https://www.socialstudies.org/resources/notable

I found two of my favorite award-winning children's books from NCSS online:

- *Rachel: The Story of Rachel Carson.* **Amy Ehrlich. Illustrated by Wendell Minor. Harcourt Children's Books. 32pp. Trade ISBN 0-15-216227-5, $16.00.**
  Rachel was born with a sense of wonder and an intense curiosity encouraged by her mother. Her exploration and writings about the natural world eventually helped launch an environmental movement.

- *The Library of Alexandria.* **Kelly Trumble. Illustrated by Robina MacIntyre Marshall. Clarion Books. Trade ISBN 0-395-75832-7, $17.00.**

  The Library of Alexandria had a collection that spanned astronomy, geography, mathematics, and medicine, making it a wonder of the ancient world. Text and illustrations of this book make the library's creation and demise come to life.

The National Science Teachers Association (NSTA) is an organization of science education professionals and has as its purpose the stimulation, improvement, and coordination of science teaching and learning. It has collaborated with the Children's Book Council on this bibliographic project since 1973. The review panel they appoint looks at both content and presentation. Selection is based generally on the following criteria:

- book has substantial science content;
- information is clear, accurate, and up to date;
- theories and facts are clearly distinguished;
- facts are not oversimplified to the point where the information is misleading;
- generalizations are supported by facts and significant facts are not omitted; and
- books are free of gender, ethnic, and socioeconomic bias.

The panel also uses rigorous selection guidelines relating to the presentation of material, including: logical presentation and a clear sequence of ideas; appropriate content level for the intended audience; compatible text and illustrations; illustrations that are accurate representations in size, color, and scale; appropriate trim size and format of the book for the subject and audience; and well-organized layout that advances the text. http://www.nsta.org/publications/ostb/ostb2005.aspx

The 2004 outstanding Science Trade Book:

- *The Boy Who Drew Birds: A Story of John James Audubon.* **Jacqueline Davies. Illustrated by Melissa Sweet. Houghton Mifflin Company. 32pp. Trade ISBN 0-618-24343-7, $15.**

  This beautifully illustrated book focuses on the young John Audubon's interest in migrating birds and depicts his attempts to determine whether some birds return to the same nest each spring. The book nicely blends historical information with a description of the process a naturalist goes through to investigate a "mystery" of nature.

Figure 5.6 Major Organizations that Evaluate Quality Picture Books for Children

In my approach to the selection of texts, I found it valuable to refer to the tripartite model for determining how easy or difficult a particular text is to read, which the Common Core State Standards New York State adopted in 2011. In addition to the quantitative aspects of text complexity that are measurable by computer software, such as word length or frequency and sentence length, the tripartite model takes into account qualitative and reader task dimensions. Four research-based qualitative factors that depend on the relation of the text to a reader's knowledge/experiences include: (a) levels of meaning (literary texts) or purpose (informational texts); (b) structure (from low or conventional to high or nonconventional); (c) language conventionality and clarity; and (d) knowledge demands of the text.

In sum, the trade books and picture books that I favor are content rich; address a wider range of experiences associated with class, color, gender, language, culture, and special needs; are of high literary quality; and have the potential to sustain the interest of children and adults over a five-day period and more. They also serve a very important role in assisting second-career teacher candidates to learn about the children and situations they are likely to encounter in the public schools in New York City, and to become more world-minded in a global city where the world resides.

Learning to Read through a Literature-based Approach

Goldman and Wiley (2004) report that well-established empirical findings for cognitive studies of reading comprehension indicate that the form and content of written texts have an impact on how readers read, understand, remember, and learn from them. Moreover, there is a relation among genre, content, and structure such that genre influences structure, and differences in structure imply different relationships among ideas in the text. A common narrative or rhetorical structure follows a pattern similar to this one: the occurrence of a problem that protagonists attempt to resolve and a series of episodes that are causally related, where one episode may be a precondition for another, though not necessarily chronologically related. By comparison, the broader structure of nonfiction text is more complex, which is why I chose to emphasize informational picture books that are written in a narrative format.

In their review of research on text structure and the physical presentation of text and their relation to reading comprehension, Dickson, Simmons, and

Kameenui (1998) found three convergent areas of evidence that have implications for teaching and teacher preparation:

• Well-presented physical text facilitates reading comprehension.
• Text structure and student awareness of text structure are highly related to reading comprehension.
• Explicit instruction in the physical presentation of text and/or text structure facilitates reading comprehension.

Chartier's (1995) analysis focuses attention on other physical qualities of text. For example, one notable feature of children's literature in the United States is that, in general, it is considered a work of art: beautiful, of high quality, often containing reproductions of well-known works of art, if not originals, and, not surprisingly, very costly in comparison with didactic materials found in schools throughout the Americas. These factors suggest that expensive books were not initially intended for popular consumption, but with a shift in emphasis since the 1980s, literature is more accessible now in school and classroom libraries. Even so, the number of books published annually with a broader representation of characters, settings, and situations, is relatively miniscule, though there are more books available than most teachers are familiar with, especially the new Latinx canon.

Historically, books representative of a wider range of experiences and children in a wider range of colors than ever before emerged as a consequence of the Civil Rights Movement of the 1960s. These included picture books with stories that portrayed a range of differences in experiences based on socioeconomic class, culture, language, gender, and race, by authors and illustrators who were similarly diverse. These differences were commonly found in families within large, urban neighborhoods as opposed to the "white," suburban, upper middle-class families represented, for example, in the *Dick and Jane* readers of the 1940s and 1950s. When books of this type had images and stories, for example about African Americans, many were derogatory and racist, reflecting the beliefs and values of the times; or people of color were simply whitewashed out of the narrative, suggesting that they were of negligible social value. I have introduced examples of some of these books in my courses as a way to explore books as cultural products that reflect the times in which they were published, and why one should always take notice of the date of publication in relation to the content of the text, as a way to situate it historically. I have also introduced books by socially conscious authors, for example Ezra Jack Keats, who published *My Dog Is Lost* in

1960, which is recognized as the first children's book in which the main character is a Puerto Rican boy who is new to the city.

Still the larger problem remains that of gaining access to books of literary quality, which incorporate themes, settings, characters, and situations that are part of the human experience that children in New York City public schools find engaging, both in terms of the content and the language. I have built a personal collection guided by multiple criteria for quality such as recommendations of various professional organizations, acknowledged authorities on the subject, and what rings true to me given my experiences, and that I have an emotional connection to. How I experience a particular book will shape how I introduce it in class, and I know from experience that my passion is also contagious. Major bookstores in the United States carry very little of what I consider to be authentic children's literature in Spanish and English, although there is a growing U.S. market in children's books that teach Spanish to mainstream English speakers. I have been able to locate books for my collection online, as well as at local bookstores and at conferences at major professional organizations and the International Books for Young Children.

Additionally, few current structures allow for the type of intensive experience working with children and texts that teachers suggest is warranted to develop needed expertise, or at least understanding. This structural problem is often hidden from view and assumed benign, even while shaping what is possible in classrooms that are often designed institutionally to discourage attention to real social issues and focus them instead on the less socioemotional, more technical mechanics of reading (Berchini, 2016).

Learning to Teach through a Literature-based Approach

The origins, historical purposes, and uses of children's literature (in its various modalities) concern teaching life lessons and socializing children to the rituals, practices, and values of community life, even though the uses of these texts, in particular, and texts in general, have always been multiple and changing (Chartier, 1995). Sonia Nieto (1983, 1993) was among the first to call attention to the representation of Latinx people (Puerto Ricans, in particular) in children's literature that she studied as cultural objects. Martínez-Roldán (2013) builds on Nieto to examine the responses of Latinx children who attend school in the U.S. southwest to literature with themes and characters they can relate to within discussion groups in bilingual classrooms.

However, in studies that are closest to my interest, DeNicolo and Franquiz (2006) use children's literature as a cultural tool for pre- and in-service teacher preparation in bilingual contexts; and Nathenson-Mejias and Escamilla (2003) found that using Latinx children's literature in a university-based teacher education program may benefit both teacher candidates and their students. This study documents that the use of Latinx children's literature in field experiences helps teacher candidates get background knowledge of the culture, traditions, language, and issues surrounding Latinx people in the United States and the elementary school students with whom they will be working: Thus, class discussions over literary texts that represent a broad range of human experiences; the way different people/children experience the world (e.g., traditions, struggle, injustice, change), and that challenge myths and stereotypes, build relevant background knowledge, and broaden participants' personal perspectives and understanding of cultures different from their own.

Through teaching as research (see Smagorinsky, 1995) I have discovered the many possibilities that the teaching of children's literature presents as instructor of children's literature in our childhood education program. I found similar patterns of responses to those that Nathenson-Mejias and Escamilla (2003) describe. Bruner (1996) reminds us that intersubjective understandings lie at the heart of the teaching-learning process and the mediation of learning. Hades (1997) elaborates through the lens of multiculturalism (analogous to inter-subjective understandings that Bruner references). According to Hades, multiculturalism "is a perspective we take to our reading to understand how race, class and gender mean in the stories we interpret. Our culture has taught us that there is meaning in the identity of someone as black or white, female or male, poor or rich; they are signs to be interpreted" (p. 241). In their responses to children's literature adults or children reveal these understandings.

Situating herself as a student of social practice in schools, Rockwell (2005) hones in on the transactional or discursive process of making texts accessible and meaningful in the classroom. Rockwell describes it as a negotiated accomplishment that involves the mutual influence of texts, oral and written language practices, and beliefs and values in real classrooms. I would add that in these guided transactions that involve the negotiation of meanings of books that are intended for children to read, adult guides should allow children to lead the way, as Wolf (2004) suggests. Initially, the teacher/adult guide may briefly take the lead as a way to encourage or provoke children's reactions to what they "see, hear, feel" as the teacher reads, and as the learner gains confidence, the adult follows their lead to gain access to insights that hint at the learner's understandings and experiences in their social worlds from what they say. For the same reason, discussions of children's literature in teacher education are powerful means, first to learn and then to mediate understandings that teacher candidates have of their students' social worlds. Given the level of conversations that the negotiation of meaning that children's literature makes possible, some professionals I know from Latin America and Spain avoid the term "children's literature," preferring the simpler and more accurate term "literature," and I can understand why.

In Shelby Wolf's 2004 book on teaching children's literature, which course participants found illuminating and engaging, Wolf advises teachers to go beyond an exclusive focus on literary analysis and combine several different types of analyses such as (a) genetic criticism or a focus on the author, (b) formal criticism with specific attention to the structure of the text, (c) text to text criticism that focuses on how one text fits within the larger body of literature, (d) transactional criticism with an eye on the reader's interaction with the text, and (e) sociocultural criticism that examines cultural, political, and sociohistorical perspectives. I followed Wolf's advice when I introduced three of my favorite Ana Maria Machado books: *Nina Bonita*, *Me in the Middle*, and *From Another World*, deepening my understanding of this selection by beginning with background information on the author obtained from the internet. The chronology that I developed as a teaching tool and as a way to illustrate how to approach the study of one author, combines words and images, and key quotes that give an insight to Machado's stance in the world and to stories with social messages (*From Another World*; *Nina Bonita*) and strong female characters (*Me in the Middle*). This also gives the learner (whether adult or a child) something to think about, and facilitates comprehension as they listen to them read loud or read independently. It also transforms an author from a name to remember to someone with whom to share a long conversation. That is how I feel about Ana Maria Machado.

Learning in a Community of Practice

During planning meetings with colleagues as the fall 2008 semester was about to begin, I had a concern that I dared not make public at the time: I wondered if it would be possible to prepare novices to put knowledge into practice in a college-based first semester methods course organized as a community of practice, as preparation for second semester supervised clinical practice in a low-performing school. I was motivated to address the "enactment" problem that results from talking about teaching rather than "doing" teaching, an elusive goal in college-based teacher preparation. It also explains the urgency I feel for assuring that novices benefit from their introductory ten-hour supervised clinical experiences in schools in low-income communities, during the semester. Consequently, I made the decision to organize my section of "developmental reading" as a community of practice (Lave & Wenger, 1991; Lave, 1996; Brown, Collins & Duguid, 1989), determined to prepare accomplished adults for their first full-day clinical experiences in semester two.

Lave explains understandings developed through anthropological cross-cultural studies of informal learning. Accordingly, learning is not a process of socially shared cognition that results in the internalization of knowledge by individuals, a view that remains dominant in formal learning settings, including college-based teacher preparation. Learning is a process of becoming a member of a sustained community of practice. Developing an identity as a member of a community (in our case, as adult learners who are learning to become teachers) and becoming knowledgeably part of the same process, with the former motivating, shaping, and giving meaning to the latter (Lave & Wenger, 1991). Brown, Collins, and Duguid (1989) elaborate: learning occurs as people participate in shared endeavors with others, with all playing active, but often asymmetrical, roles in sociocultural activity. Both mature members of the community and less mature members are conceived as active; no role has all the responsibility for knowing or directing, and no role is, by definition, passive. In my estimation, this is precisely the type of learning community that a first semester course on developmental reading should strive for in preparing second career teaching aspirants to teach high utility core literacy practices. As Shulman explains: "In professional education, it is insufficient to learn for the sake of knowledge and understanding alone; one learns in order to engage in practice. Professional education involves teaching ideas, facts and principles so that they can contribute to skilled professional practice" (2005, p. 18).

This view of learning professional practice makes sense to me and is compatible with the views of a growing number of scholars who advocate a "practice-based" approach to teacher preparation (cf. Ball & Forzani, 2011). The practice-based approach that I favor as an educator integrates knowing with doing; more precisely, the integration of knowing, acting, and being (Dall'Alba & Barnacle, 2007). However, as Shulman also reminds us, the performance of practice must not only be skilled and theoretically grounded, it must be characterized by integrity, by a commitment to responsible, ethical service, under conditions of inherent and unavoidable uncertainties. Thus, the views of esteemed scholars guided how I approached a new first semester developmental reading course with the ambitious goal of introducing high utility, core literacy practices to second career teaching aspirants on fast track to becoming the teacher of record.

With clarity of purpose, I embarked on a journey into the unknown, trusting that I had the power to make a difference and knowing that in daring to act, I was stretching myself, and those who joined me on this journey beyond our comfort zones. I also understood that leaving our comfort zones was a necessary first step to address the "enactment" problem that scholars identify as a serious problem in teacher preparation, and that, in turn, affects the learning experiences teachers organize for vulnerable children.

Course Overview

As an educator in a highly politicized field of study, I have spent many hours in classrooms where I have witnessed first-hand, the low-level (and boring) literacy instruction in childhood education, typically for children ages six through eleven, and in neighborhoods where many households struggle to make ends meet. Instruction in these classrooms is in stark contrast to practices and resources commonly found in public schools in more affluent neighborhoods or even in working-class communities where old public school buildings with capacity for over 1,000 children house a range of different programs. Confronting such stark educational inequalities fuels the passion and the will to act through courses that prepare second career teaching aspirants to teach the core content area of reading and language arts in under-resourced, low performing schools.

The introductory literacy courses that I have developed are informed by teacher certification requirements and best practice research that inspire new ways of thinking about teaching the core content area of English Language Arts. "Text Talk" (Beck & McKeown, 2001) by Isabel Beck and "The Role of Knowledge in Early Literacy" by Susan Neuman (2001) are scholarship that puts knowledge into practice. However, even the best of the best-practice research requires adaptation to be locally appropriate, in a policy context that has standardized and reduced the intellectual level of literacy instruction. For these reasons, the literacy courses that I have developed are also informed by teaching experiments that I organized in collaboration with classroom teachers who sought to build intellectual and cultural bridges between schools and communities to improve the teaching of literacy in high poverty schools (cf. Chapter 4).

How I teach is part of *what* I teach: (a) to learn in the community, where we are all teachers and learners, using the power of the written and spoken word and other symbolic media to develop mutually supportive relationships in a borderless social space where we are open to the influences of schools, families, and other communities of practice; (b) to experience the work of teaching as a moral act to put knowledge into practice in the interest of vulnerable children who depend on teachers to prepare them to become independent, resourceful learners; and to (c) use reading and writing as a tool to reflect on and to gain consciousness of the value of learning in and from the different experiences and perspectives of others we encounter in a borderless world. Although the Teacher Education Program that is my home institution is regulated by the State Education Department, I have some level of academic freedom to organize an instructional approach that best fits who I am and what I know. I provide a brief overview of what I now consider to be the significant moments in a fifteen-session semester teaching a new course on development reading. This overview gives a sense of my distinct approach to preparing accomplished adults to benefit from first clinical experiences.

Session One

After self-introductions, I provide a brief overview of a new course on developmental reading, including its goals, activities, and requirements. Given that a typical syllabus is now well over ten pages, I begin by providing just enough information to understand course requirements without overwhelming the group. I also want to ensure there is time for a first experience with the range of children's books in my personal collection, which are broadly representative of the diversity of the school population, and are the heart of the course. I call attention to several titles as I place books at random on table clusters to give a sense of the range of topics and genres appropriate for childhood education. There are sufficient books to enable each person to access at least three of them. We will pause to review these books before beginning our self-introductions using one of three books that motivated some second career teaching aspirants to make a "text to self" connection. This is a comprehension strategy that I borrowed from the mandated Balanced Literacy Approach. I consider this a novel (and appropriate) way to get acquainted with other members of our community, and with the books that are at the heart of teaching developmental reading.

Sessions Three and Four

In the third session I assume the role of a third grade teacher to introduce the preview lesson that prepares children for the weekly read aloud selection, *Rachel* (see Figure 5.7). I chose this picture book about a woman scientist and writer who was acknowledged as the leader of the environmental movement in the United States. The preview lesson is the first in a series of five activities that include the Interactive Read Aloud, a core practice featured in this course and in the citywide mandated reading and writing program. Holding the book so that the cover is visible to all, I call attention to the title of the book and the name of the author on the front cover, checking first to see if anyone can make sense of the words "picture book biography." If no one does, I tell them what it means and move on to examine the image of a child standing in a field where birds and trees are visible. I probe to find what learners notice before I describe what I see, hear, and feel, and invite others to share what they see, hear, and feel.

The second illustration is of a little girl in the woods in the company of her dog. She appears to notice a seashell on the ground. I probe for understanding before passing around a seashell fossil so that children may hold and examine it. Typical responses are that it looks like a seashell but feels like a rock. I name it as a seashell fossil and wonder aloud how the seashell got to be the way it is and how it got to the woods. In not explaining, the author creates an opportunity to learn from interdisciplinary connections at another time (and why I return to it in session four). The last illustration is of a woman looking under a microscope and I ask, as if talking to children, "Who do you think this woman is?" I allow a few guesses and conclude by asking the class if they are curious about and have an interest in wanting to learn about who Rachel was and why there is a book about her life.

Shifting my attention to the adults, we conclude by sharing observations on the experience before I make my thinking public (see Figure 5.8). Next, I share my preview script, a conceptual tool to think about how I want to introduce the book and a mnemonic to remember what is important, *not* to be read aloud. I conclude with a reflection on the experience, making public my thinking about what I did in relation to what I had planned to do. We close with participant comments on how the experience assists in planning their preview lesson. We break into small self-selected groups for the first planning session.

In session four I call attention to the contextual materials I used to build background knowledge on Rachel that enables the making of interdisciplinary connections. The use of contextual materials (e.g., photographs, recordings, information briefs) is an alternative approach to textual comprehension that assists English learners to make sense of written texts. Similarly, using as many of the five senses as possible also assists in making sense of experience and print. Teaching English learners requires that teachers broaden the range of symbolic media they use to assist English learners to construct and demonstrate their understandings, including performances and "visualizations." This entire sequence is a complex but accessible learning experience that yields useful practice. Similarly, session five completes a sequence that begins with a preview lesson and concludes with a four-day sequential plan focused on relevant core skills from Reading First, such as word study focused on the meaningful parts of words, e.g., microscope and telescope; the genre of biography; big ideas such as "web of life," and allowing choice in selecting favorite scenes from Rachel's story, introducing novices to teach developmental reading in high needs schools without reducing its complexity.

Session Five

We follow a similar planning cycle, preparing a preview lesson for the picture book *Nina Bonita*, a simple text that gives us much to think about and introduces literary language that English learners usually find challenging, but made accessible with visual images, e.g., of a black panther. Preparing the preview script takes into account that this is a book for younger children, which is why we pay close attention to the appropriateness of the experience, including the language we use to speak to young children, a fine balance between being age appropriate and building on children's curiosity. We also explore different ways to engage young children in displaying their understandings, through re-enactments of scenes with a repetitive refrain.

Following each demonstration, participants organize themselves into small groups to plan and decide on a common focus or adaptation of demonstrations of preview lessons, preview scripts, and four-day sequential plans focused on Reading First skills, including an assessment using the books used for class demonstrations or other choices. As course participants begin their ten-hour classroom observations required by the NYS teacher certification unit, they bring these experiences to our guided, collaborative activities, adding further depth and complexity to our understandings of the picture books we review in class: the preview lessons we develop to be locally appropriate.

Session Six

I introduce the sequential planning activity for *Rachel* (see Figure 5.8) by demonstrating how I would plan four "standards-based" mini lessons (about fifteen minutes each) on relevant skills from Reading First that are appropriate to the selection, using the instructional planning format of the school of education that I modified to fit on a standard size page, to make visible the four-day sequence to facilitate coherent planning. I advise second career teaching aspirants to come prepared to make good use of planning time as they work in small groups to develop an original or adaptations of the four-day instructional sequence that fits the read aloud selection. Core skills from Reading First include word study, vocabulary and textual, comprehension that may be demonstrated in a visualization, a performance, or a written explanation or summary.

In sum, course participants will also have multiple opportunities to observe, plan, and rehearse core practices specific to teaching reading and writing in the elementary grades that I first demonstrate or model, that they observe during their ten-hour observations in local classrooms, and that other members of our community demonstrate, in small or large groups. Over time, these learning experiences augment the number of tools and resources that first year teachers will bring to teaching literacy in underperforming schools, and that are especially relevant to the new literature-based, locally mandated balanced literacy approach in which the interactive read aloud has a prominent role. Broadening the range of symbolic media also provides English learners with a range of alternatives to display their understandings, as illustrated in the visualizations that served as a "book review" or "summary." In effect, in addition to the broad range of quality children's books that I introduce during weekly sessions, the learning experiences I organize augment the number of tools and resources new teachers will take with them to their first supervised clinical practice experience.

- **Introduce picture book:**
Rachel: The Story of Rachel Carson is a picture biography. A picture biography is a special kind of informational book. It tells the story of Rachel's life in words and pictures, but it doesn't tell all of her life. It just tells about some important parts and facts about her life. Why does that make sense—to tell only parts of her life?

- **Summarize story:**

In *The Story of Rachel Carson* we learn what Rachel enjoyed doing as a child, how she became a student of life, and the important work she did as a scientist. Rachel Carson helped to protect our family and made our home a safer place for us to live.

- **Introduce purpose:**

I am not going to read the book to you today, as I sometimes do during read aloud. We are going to preview the book together. Do you know what the word preview means? It's the kind of word that tells you what it means if you pay close attention to how it looks and how it sounds. (Call on 3.) It's important to preview informational books because they contain factual information and we don't want to miss what these books have to teach us, do we?

- **Introduce features of text:**

For the past few weeks we have been reading lots of informational picture books. What have you noticed about these books? [Prompts, as needed: "If you had to describe an informational book to someone who has never seen one, what would you tell them?" "What special features do these books have?"] Jot down responses on chart paper. Anticipated responses: Pictures on the cover, on the inside, chapter titles, words.

So, today we are going to look at some of those pictures and some of those words to prepare for listening to the story tomorrow/next week. Let's take a look at some of the pictures that help to prepare us for learning from the story.

1. Rachel looking closely at a fossil in the chapter called "The Sea Fossil 1912";
2. Rachel looking into a microscope and taking notes;
3. Rachel holding up binoculars to look at hawks.

- **Introduce specialized:**

Write each word; call attention to meaningful parts (morphology); state in ordinary language; and pass around seashell fossil (as artifact).

BIOLOGY is about the study of life, the WEB-OF-LIFE, and how all living ORGANISMS are related to one another, like a family; BIOLOGISTS study life using tools to examine living and dead organisms; they use a MICROSCOPE to study SPECIMENS we cannot see with our naked eyes; they study FOSSILS of life from long ago (demonstrate relationship among terms in visual format).

- **Sum up:**

How many of you are looking forward to listening to the story of *Rachel* tomorrow?

State in your own words what we accomplished today. (Write individual responses as collaborative summary.)

Figure 5.7 Mercado Preview Lesson for *Rachel: The Story of Rachel Carson*

RELATIONSHIPS

Teaching is based on an understanding of oneself and others, hence the heart and soul of teaching begins with relationships.

TRUST

Participation in a collaborative learning process is shared responsibility that is guided by the belief that the process will yield positive outcomes for the individual and for the collective.

PURPOSE

Teaching needs to be purposeful, from both the teacher's and learners' perspectives.

ENGAGEMENT AND CHALLENGE

The teaching educator needs to understand the array of responses to her pedagogy, the influx of new and challenging ideas and the experience of cognitive dissonance when alternative conceptions are explored through mutual engagement. Demonstrating (modeling) this type of engagement in one's own teaching can give real access to the thoughts, skills, and knowledge of experienced teachers in ways that allow adults learning to teach to learn what is involved in teaching and to make their own decisions about pedagogy. Adults learning to teach as well as teaching educators must understand how teaching practices affect their learning. Modeling does not imply mimicking or creating a template for teaching; modeling serves to make transparent the pedagogical reasons of an experienced teacher; knowing why must be linked to knowing how.

REFLECTION

Reconsidering one's actions, reframing problematic situations, mulling over the flow of suggestions, and reasoning through the implications of alternative views are the cornerstone of reflection. Thinking aloud about my pedagogy gives immediate access to my thoughts, to pedagogical reasons for activities/learning experiences I organize. The interplay between teaching and learning "in action" is difficult as the ideas, perceptions, reactions, and recognition of anticipated and unanticipated learning outcomes ebb and flow in response to the stimuli that prompt the thinking. It is fundamental that thinking be overtly demonstrated to fully appreciate the complex nature of learning about teaching.

RISK TAKING

Learning about teaching requires a pushing of the boundaries of practice to encourage seeing and understanding from a variety of vantage points. New ways of seeing and understanding practice become possible through the experience of discomfort of being less certain about the unfolding events within a teaching–learning episode. The experience of risk taking substantially broadens one's understanding of both the teaching and learning, cognitively and affectively. Risk taking on the part of all participants involves pursuing the implementation of strategies that cater to diversity or learning needs within the teaching environment.

Figure 5.8 A Pedagogy for Teaching Teaching
Source: Loughran (1997).

Conclusion

Through collaborative experiences in self-selected affinity groups followed by whole class debriefing and discussion, second career teaching aspirants put into practice core reading and writing practices appropriate to a first semester course. They include: (a) displaying professional judgment in selecting quality children's literature (picture and chapter books) containing themes, situations and characters that are inclusive of a diverse school population, and content worthy of instructional time; (b) using a model to develop an original or adapted script for previewing one book, and preparing a twenty-minute book introduction for children in grades one to three or three to six based on the script; (c) designing four sequential twenty-minute skills-based lessons guided by the English Language Arts Standards; and (d) an assessment to gauge comprehension of the select text that combines visual symbols and words to capture a central theme or idea (a visualization). Over time, participants become increasingly independent, rehearsing or trying out practices/ideas of their own initiative, in spaces that feel safe (not always in class); and soliciting feedback from peers. They also seek out timely assistance from their instructor, individually or in small groups, or via electronic mail; and if they do not I make myself a presence through electronic mails, brief exchanges in class, and sometimes by phone, because sustaining engagement in the process is as important as the final product. In effect, what I notice are signs of a shift in participation, from participating as a "student" to participating as a "professional," as I will discuss in the next chapter. In

Chapter 6, I examine how teacher candidates assess their preparedness in organizing and assessing intellectually and emotionally challenging instruction that is responsive to the emotional and intellectual needs of diverse English learners through a grade appropriate, literature-based approach that sustains children's interest over twenty-minute instructional segments that conclude with a written assessment.

Teaching as Learning in Practice

Our work as educators is not without history. Maintaining a connection to this history by making it part of our ongoing reflections about teaching, learning, and schools, and its broader social context within our gaze, provides us with larger sets of possibilities for our practice (Perrone, 1998). This is possible when reflection leads to critical consciousness; that is, coming to terms with the reality that teaching and teacher education are inherently political and, as such, they reflect conflicting values about the purposes, roles, and content of schooling in the twenty-first century (Cochran-Smith & Zeichner, 2005). How we navigate these turbulent waters to attain valued goals yields important lessons that may inform the preparation of adults who are recruited to teach vulnerable children who attend under-resourced and under-performing schools.

In this chapter I embark upon a retrospective analysis, seeking to understand how second career teaching aspirants experienced a practice-based approach to learning to teach "developmental reading," in a course organized as a community of practice. In particular, I seek to understand whether at the end of fifteen-session semester teaching aspirants perceive that they are prepared to benefit from supervised clinical practice experiences in the low-scoring schools where they are expected to teach "lessons" in the mandated literature-based Balanced Literacy program combined with the Reading First approach to early reading instruction. The perception of preparedness will no doubt shape the confidence of these second career teaching aspirants and, in turn, their confidence and willingness to make the most of unexpected opportunities to engage in "real" classroom teaching during weekly supervised clinical experiences. In effect, it is this perception of feeling prepared to teach that is what I seek to develop through course activities.

It is also important to acknowledge that faculty is expected to organize course content in accordance with current policies and practices of the teacher education program where we reside and the state agencies that regulate these programs. However, as I have described in previous chapters, these policies and practices also change to reflect new state certification requirements informed by relevant professional organizations. This has been the case with the International Reading Association (now the International Literacy Association or ILA) and the professional preparation standards of the Interstate New Teacher Assessment and Support Consortium (InTASC). This explains why I organize course outcomes to emphasize "knowledge, skills and dispositions" needed to teach developmental reading in "diverse, inclusive urban elementary schools." Pre- and in-service teachers are well aware that those are the categories that will to be used to evaluate them at our institution.

Artifacts generated from teaching from 2008 to 2010 include, but are not limited to: (a) ongoing and summative course reflections, (b) session notes, summaries, and worksheets, (c) personal notes and emails received from course participants during and after the semester has ended; and (d) comments on faculty evaluations. In addition, data are examined at three points in time: during the semester, at the end of semester, and since the semester ended in December 2010. I undertook previous analyses as I prepared documentation for my promotion to full professor in 2004. At that time, I analyzed data over a ten-year period (from 1993–2003), contrasting course evaluations that reduced my teaching to numerical averages that did not always meet departmental norms, to qualitative data derived primarily from session logs and summative reflections that rendered a more nuanced portrait of our teaching transactions. The intent, in this case, was to re-present my practice to those who would be voting on whether I merited promotion to full professor in a service one institution where teaching is a priority. Data generated from final reflections suggest what I consider to be significant learning outcomes for a course on language and literacy from the spring 2002 semester. Student evaluations include the following testimonials:

> The video [of the fourth grader reading] helped me realize … that teachers should not label or prejudge a child too early because we can be surprised by our students. This also made me realize that a teacher must try out all possibilities before saying anything about what a child can or cannot do.
>
> The article [by Taylor & Dorsey-Gaines, 1988] made me realize that even though a family's financial situation is unstable they may still be trying hard to provide reading material for their children. It also opened my eyes to the variety of types and uses of literacy found in households.
>
> The most important thing I got out of this class is something that may be difficult for me to explain—it's the way I am thinking … I have always been interested in the why's of people, as far as behaviors and learning. I am now very interested in how we learn language.

Most of my students are English learners. I have learned to look at the whole picture: Understanding the learner's background, experiences, environment, and previous knowledge.

The greatest insights I have gained from this class have come from these classroom exercises. It is one thing to read about a theory, but it is another to be a part of an experience.

I like how our class was free to discuss. I felt we had a good relationship and we have been each other's support teams. Teachers need to discuss these issues and share their experiences. We can and did learn from each other. I am glad to be working with other professionals and people that care as much about children as I do.

In sharing the children's writing, it was fascinating that there was such range of abilities within the same grade level.

Some comments were more critical of course content and processes, as this range illustrates: (a) learning from a nontraditional pedagogy; (b) lack of specificity in stating course objectives; (c) labor intensive course assignments requiring peer collaborations; (d) level of difficulty of course readings; and (e) ambiguity of grading practices. Based on my analysis of students' reflective writing, I offered this explanation in my 2004 promotion documents:

> Teaching for social justice requires us to question the conventional—conventional thinking about how children and adult learners learn, what children and adult learners know and how teachers at all levels teach. There is also urgency in knowing, "What evidence is there that what I do as a teaching educator contributes to the development of understandings, practices, and dispositions teacher candidates need to teach vulnerable children?" "How do I use what I learn from teaching to inform my pedagogy in subsequent courses?" Traditional teacher evaluation, while useful, is not designed to provide the type of timely information that I seek and need to address these critical needs.

Although I knew the practices that were important to introduce in a first-semester methods course, I was unable to see clearly the different forces that shape course experiences until I engaged in cultural historical activity theory (CHAT), a more comprehensive analysis, as I will explain. CHAT is a practical theory that creates consciousness of the interplay of influences, so that we may respond appropriately (Daniels, 2007).

Moreover, although I was fairly free to meet state certification requirements as I deemed appropriate, increasingly teacher candidates compared the content, process, and difficulty level of courses, by different instructors in the same department, and were not reluctant to express concerns or disagreements. The one comment that was most concerning related to course workload. This complaint was understandable when I step back to consider how a social justice agenda driven by the sense of urgency that I felt as a professional whose work has consequences for vulnerable children. My oversight came in ignoring how the workload required by this agenda affected the lives of graduate students (mostly women) who work during the day, enroll in two or more evening courses, and have families to care for when they return home at night. I was challenged to find a way to make the workload manageable, while addressing the social justice agenda that guided professional practice.

When I reread the writings of course participants at different points in time during the semester, I experience a gamut of emotions that trigger vivid recollections of moments of teaching within a changing emotional landscape. Now, with new theoretical tools, combined with flashes of insight that occur spontaneously in the process of narrating lived experience, I am able to do a new reading of what escaped me in the moment or that I may have interpreted differently. This process offers a more complex analysis of lived experience in a first-semester methods course that prepares novices to teach reading and writing to learn in a course organized as a community of practice.

Now in retirement, minus the burdens of a twenty-one-credit course load, there is urgency in knowing what we accomplished together, through our mutual influence during a brief fifteen-session semester that may inform the professional community and advance our conversation on how to develop "embodied knowing." Rigor in this analysis means accounting for all sources of influence on how we teach since the passage of the No Child Left Behind Act in 2002, the most influential and controversial piece of federal legislation on what and how we teach developmental reading and, consequently, on what teacher candidates learn.

Therefore, in this chapter I reexamine evidence for how a practiced-based approach to preparing novices to teach developmental reading, in a course organized as a community of practice, shapes how we engage with practices that are key components of the mandated citywide literacy approach, as is the Interactive Read Aloud. The added layer of complexity is that the course needs to focus on instruction in schools attended by children (predominantly English learners) from families with incomes that fall below the poverty level. I also examine influences that shaped and changed how we cooperated and collaborated to attain goals that appeared to be beyond our reach.

Unlike my first years of teaching, my last three years of teaching before retirement included enhanced knowledge, experience, and values, which I used to shape an approach to a first semester methods course in developmental reading for accomplished career changers on an accelerated timeframe, from 2008 to 2010. I did so with a new urgency and immediacy, searching for evidence to support what I assumed to be true: It is possible to promote the development of core reading practices in a fifteen-session college/university-based course.

I come to this perspective as someone who has engaged in teaching as research for close to three decades, because it is a quest to find out how learners are constructing their own understandings of what we expose them to in our courses (Duckworth, 1986), what is also referred to as a constructivist view of teaching. After all these years, Duckworth's words still speak to me: "I like to find ways into a subject that will catch everybody's interest ... and to find ways to get them talking about what they think; to shake up things they thought they knew; to get people wrapped up in figuring something out together, without needing anything from me" (p. 120).

However, the quest to understand the complexities that the teaching–learning process includes, but goes beyond, the immediate transaction, to the invisible forces that shape what we do. As Daniels (2007) argues, such an analysis requires three lenses. One lens zooms out to capture the larger system in which practice is situated: the social, institutional, and political forces that shape instructional practice in an ecological niche in which "everything is connected to everything else" (Wideen, Mayer-Smith & Moon, 1998, p. 168). Another lens zooms in to examine the relation between teaching and learning.

According to Loughran (2007), studying teaching and teacher education practices (STTEP) is "a way of purposefully examining the relationship between teaching and learning so that alternative perspectives on the intentions and outcomes might be better realized" (p. 174). Through STTEP, a teacher educator may then become better informed about not only the nature of learning from a given pedagogic situation, but also the possibilities for developing appropriate alternatives for future experiences. Consequently, when I frame my research as the study of teaching and teacher educator practices, I do so out of the need to better prepare novices to work in the best interests of vulnerable children as a social good (Van Manen, 1990). The Lat-Crit (Latinx-Critical) lens makes visible social and structural forces that shape relationships of power between/among course participants, when these include members of underrepresented groups who bring nonmainstream perspectives to teaching and teacher preparation (The Latina Feminist Group, 2001).

Combining these three frameworks enables me to explain rather than simply describe a complexity that is inherent in the teaching–learning process, as a Latinx teacher educator who brings nonmainstream perspectives to a presumably mainstream practice setting. Although analysis is focused on the last three years before retirement, I recall Dewey's (1938) reminder that life is a series of experiences in which all past experiences shape future experiences, as these change over time. This process awakens past experiences (opening old wounds and new appreciations of what we accomplished) as the past comes into the present, in what Stern (in Pinnegar & Hamilton, 2009) conceptualizes as the present moment. Accordingly, present moments are the smallest units of lived experience containing a beginning, a middle, and an end. This unification of experience accounts for why we are aware and conscious of experiences we feel intellectually and emotionally as a whole.

As a theoretical tool, the present moment allows us to bring to mind our lived experiences, experiencing them in the here-and-now, reinterpreted with new theoretical tools and what we have learned from these experiences. Present moments allow us to learn anew from experience, as Dewey (1938) suggested. Stern argues that to understand practice and to learn from experience we must conceive of present moments as being in a kind of dialogic equilibrium with the past and the future. With time to ponder and make new sense of experience, I begin to see what previously escaped me, as new understandings come into focus and retheorizing begins. Thus, all previous analyses are mirrored in this new analysis.

Data Sources

Sources of data for this retrospective analysis are derived from the fall 2008 to the fall of 2010. I use faculty evaluation data to select three of seven sections to focus on for this study: the first section in the fall 2008 (4.65); the last section in the fall 2010 (5.93); and the one in between, in the spring 2009 (5.19). I re-examine qualitative data for sixty-seven mature, accomplished adult learners who bring a broad range of experiences into teaching. Qualitative data include ongoing and summative reflections, including comments on student evaluations, notes and embedded writings from collaborative learning experiences, and electronic mails during and months or years after the semester ended. In general, these artifacts result from efforts to understand and offer and/or seek timely support for candidates' concerns and interests, and to modify or rethink my pedagogical approach and assignments. As a priority, I focus on the smallest units of language that carry meaning: words.

Now with time to engage in a deeper analysis than was previously possible and with heightened consciousness of the potential value of this new analysis to inform conversations on the process of teacher preparation under different conditions, I review evidence to support the claim that it is possible to prepare novices for second semester supervised clinical experiences in a first-semester, college-based course organized as a community of practice. This analysis takes into account the institutional, historical, and cultural forces that shape how novices may teach literacy in under-performing schools in low-income communities, and how socially conscious teachers may navigate these turbulent waters to act in the best interests of vulnerable children.

Findings on Learning in a Community of Practice

Promoting the Integration of Knowing, Acting, and Being

Guided by the best of intentions, I did not anticipate the emotional response that accomplished adults expressed verbally and nonverbally as they entered a pedagogical space that was both unfamiliar and intimidating, unlike what they had known as college students, or experienced in other courses that they were currently taking. For adults who had successfully navigated traditional academic settings independently, the interdependence that I required did not come easily. Therefore, as instructor I had to fix my gaze on a changing emotional landscape, reading with great care interactions during the session and written reflections after each session, and, in between, insisting on making my presence felt, whether or not it was solicited. As scholars (Britzman, 2013) predict, some experiences, more than others, heightened tensions and affected engagement, as did professional readings that used unfamiliar ways of talking about literacy or presented unfamiliar viewpoints that challenged participants' assumptions and viewpoints, as the reading on class-based differences in children's development elicited. Although most appeared willing to explore these ideas, a few resisted what did not fit with what they knew or had experienced as students.

I lived with this heightened sense of uncertainty over the course of each semester, an uncertainty that Shulman (2005) illuminates. Although I acted with judgment and awareness that my actions as instructor have consequences for adult learners I encounter each semester, in truth I have no control over how they will react. These uncertainties that Shulman describes shaped the relationships I developed with the adults each semester, in a landscape of emotions. The course intimidated some, angered a few, and earned the trust of the majority to teach them what they needed to learn. Variations across sections, as Shulman believes, are the products of who we are, who the students are, and the content of instruction and the social/institutional context in which these exchanges take place. This diversity suggests the antiquatedness of the idea that we can standardize instruction across different sections of the same course. There were as many differences across sections during a semester as there were across different semesters, and individual members of the collective always have uniquely different experiences.

Our experiences contributed to a sense of community once participants felt comfortable soliciting and offering support from other members of our community as a professional community of practice (Shultz & Ravitch, 2013). Yet differences surfaced within and across the three sections of developmental reading as each individual member of the collective always has a unique experience. In sum, organizing the course as a community of practice multiplied the number of resources that individuals had access to. Through collective effort, the group could accomplish challenging work beyond what a single individual is able to do alone.

However, the first experience in the fall of 2008 was also a journey into the unknown. I needed to be hyper-vigilant for verbal and gestural indicators requiring attention or action, especially during the critical first weeks of the semester when participants began to build relationships of trust with peers as they prepared for collective activities that required collaboration and cooperation. Initially there were understandable tensions, but these subsided over time as most participants gave themselves to the process as they began to experience the benefits that collaboration yielded in comparison with working independently. As the words of course participants reveal, participating in a community of practice proved effective in the long run, although there were individual differences in what each one was able to accomplish, and might be expected when everyone enters the process in a different place. Even so, by the end of the semester, an increase in the level of confidence (or less uncertainty) was noticeable as participants began to appropriate practices they would enact in the schools where they would soon become the teacher of record. As some admitted, this preparation provided one of the benefits of learning to teach (and to becoming a teacher) in a supportive community of practice where we all served as resources for one another.

However, attaining these outcomes demands that instructors remain watchful, monitoring progress and intervening to offer support and sustain the focus individually, in small groups, and collectively. Because of the unobtrusive and multiple ways that I responded to the actions and words of participants, I remain unsure as to how they understood my role as instructor, (organizing activities, observing, and responding to needs) and as co-participant.

By far, the biggest challenge I confronted was time, a precious and limited commodity that working in a community of practice requires in a first-semester methods course. Meeting for 150 minutes each week was simply not enough time to respond to ongoing concerns and to introduce, demonstrate, explain, and reflect on practice to deepen understanding of the thinking behind what appears to be a simple practice, such as the preview lesson. Mindful of these constraints, I remained a presence through electronic mails, meetings, and phone conversations. Not surprisingly, on rare occasion I heard some say that they were "teaching themselves," an expression I have heard over the years, in part because I monitor the time spent on recitation to allow for demonstrations of and conversations about practice. In sum, the evidence that teaching to learn generates a sense of community suggests that even accomplished adults who have experienced success through traditional arrangements where it all depends on the teacher (Britzman, 1999/2003) give themselves to and gain from a process that represents another way of learning. The following testimonials from student evaluations suggests that the course both succeeded and could have worked better toward the end of developing a community of practice:

1. We all came from different backgrounds and, as such, we all have different, great ideas. It can make teaching and lesson planning better.
2. I really enjoyed my in-class experiences with classmates during the work group assignments, especially because it gave me the opportunity to open up and express myself . . . and gave me a sense of security about what I was doing.
3. I am learning a lot from the different experiences and backgrounds of others, drawing upon other people's knowledge and skills to enhance my own.
4. I had little faith in collaborative group projects. I've been astounded with my group's collaborative work on the curriculum project. It's like having four brains in your head.

5. It was definitely a struggle to work with two or three other students who have different opinions on how to approach the preview lesson, but they offered some great ideas that helped shift my point of view.

6. In the end, I really appreciated this class not only because of the things I learned, but because ... everyone's voice was heard and praised, everyone's uniqueness celebrated ... a great model of how to set up a classroom. Collaborative planning has sharpened listening skills and working in a team environment (spring 2009).

7. While a lot of my learning this semester has taken place in the classroom, I have learned quite a bit from other experiences ... I try to read as much as I can ... both online and in books. I also tutor children in a second grade class.

8. It has been interesting to observe Readers Workshop, Writers Workshop and Word Study. Reading with the children ... invaluable. Reading about how children read is completely different from actually seeing them read in person.

Some students, apparently expecting a more professorial teaching approach, found fault with the course and its instructor for not playing a stronger role:

> Great human being but not qualified to teach in college. She did not provide this class with the materials, resources, and skills useful to complete the curriculum project.
>
> I appreciated class opinions of which standards are more important but would benefit from more professor dictated instruction.

Enacting Core Practice

As the following participant comments suggest, it is possible to support pre-service teachers to enact core literacy practices of high utility in an introductory methods course organized as a community of practice. Ideally, this development should continue under supervised clinical experiences that offer the opportunity to engage in practice one full day a week. However, these outcomes require that clinical faculty—people hired into instructional rather than research positions, and having teaching rather than publication requirements—put aside regular and consistent time for engaging in informed practice, ranging from participating in the weekly read aloud, to planning and enacting an engaging preview lesson that leaves children wanting to hear more. Developing fluency and confidence in these basic practices requires time and support from all who supervise teacher candidates in their placements and dedication. It also demands hard work on the part of novices who take advantage of every opportunity that presents itself, sometimes unexpectedly, to practice their craft, as shown in an electronic mail I received four months after the spring 2009 semester ended. Student evaluations included the following observations, organized into general comments, attention to instructional materials, knowledge of learners, changes in self-knowledge, and changes in professional knowledge.

General Comments

Observing you as you introduce your preview lesson on *Rachel*, and then executing our own lesson with *Nina Bonita* was effective. It allowed me to see the process and to find my own voice.

The class was structured like a balanced literacy workshop. The professor modeled what we are supposed to do, and we get to experience the classroom from a student's perspective.

I've also learned to be realistic in planning. If I keep in mind that it's only twenty minutes then I can plan accordingly and realistically.

My favorite part of the class was presenting ideas to the whole class . . . I get very nervous when speaking in front of others . . . but I was able to present my posters and visualizations . . . like a teacher.

Observing classmates, making attempts at lesson plans, and taking feedback.

Adapting books for special learners was a completely new concept but will make such a difference in my teaching if I ever have visually impaired students, also useful for English Learners.

I borrow ideas from my Saturday class and try them out in my teaching practices the following week.

When I think back over the whole course, the most effective exercises were the ones that allowed me to see and do the practice of teaching.

This course has taught me many different ways of presenting seemingly boring material. Visualizations on the Machado books were amazing. These are the things I loved and enjoyed . . . a lasting impact on my career as an educator.

I walk away from this class with the ability to say that I have written a lesson plan . . . also how to have "Text Talk" and read aloud in class. I have a long way to go before I consider myself good at them, but I consider it a step in the right direction.

The professor's style of teaching is enlightening, well planned and very informative. . . . She brings passion to the classroom about teaching and fosters that concept on to her students. Personally, she is a role model because she is the first Latinx professor I've ever seen or had and she teaches from her heart and inspiration.

I am writing to share a great experience I had this week. ... I am in a third grade classroom every Tuesday, in East Harlem. Yesterday was my second day and the plan was for me to go over a read aloud with the teacher. ... She wasn't there and the student teacher was a little panicky ... so I offered to do *I'm in Charge of Celebrations* by Byrd Baylor. She was thrilled I had the children define celebration, then look over the cover of the book and tell me what they noticed and why. I prompted them on the vocabulary and, surprisingly, one student knew what beargrass is. I remembered the read aloud I observed last semester and had the children "turn and talk" to their neighbor. I asked questions throughout the lesson, and often followed up with, "What made you say that?" After twenty minutes ... I had to have an independent writing piece that flowed out of the story. After we had a great "share" session about the triple rainbow day, I ran with it and rolled into the writing piece.

There were fewer, though no less insightful, comments on instructional materials, knowledge of learners, self-knowledge and professional knowledge, but equally insightful.

Instructional Materials

Made me aware of the importance of teaching reading through the use of words and stories but also through the study of multicultural literature. It is important to read stories that children can relate to and see themselves in. We live in a multicultural world.

Beck's Text Talk ... was a turning point for me because instead of discussing teaching reading and writing on a theoretical level, they offered techniques and strategies on how to teach reading, and how students respond to certain techniques.

I have fallen in love all over again with children's books as a result of being in this class and I enjoy sharing them with my family and friends.

Knowledge of Learners

One cannot approach teaching reading and writing without first getting to know the child as an individual. Studying Teddy's early written work, and his usage of African American Vernacular English (AAVE), made me think about my own family.

Sharing your experiences with sixth graders offered valuable insights into what motivates students to learn, and illustrates the leaps and bounds students can make in writing if they, and their teacher, are committed to it. I definitely see the benefits of not speaking down to students, of using college words and teaching research strategies used in college writing. It sets the bar high ... develop confidence.

Anecdotes you shared were inspiring and sometimes sad. This is definitely a technique I will take with my kids at home and as a teacher.

Watching *The Sign*, then reading students' actual works and conferencing had a profound effect on me personally. Not only did it show the impact of words and how they can affect lives, it put into perspective the many roles of the teacher. The voices of the children come through their writing and how the teacher approaches the corrections for the child can impact positively or negatively.

Changes in Self-Knowledge

This course has taught me about the strengths that I can bring to the classroom. I believe that my knowledge of and experiences with AAVE will aid in my ability to reach young writers who speak AAVE to become successful writers.

In this class (and only in this class) I felt pushed to look farther into myself to answer some of the questions.

Overall, I see the big picture of where I am going with this class, but now I need to focus on the details that will make one more effective.

I am learning how to make room for other people's ideas and perspectives when I already have my own plan or ideas in mind. Also learning how important it is to clarify something before moving on to the next step.

Changes in Professional Knowledge

Being introduced to the English Language Arts curriculum and standards, and "Put Reading First" guide for teaching children to read have been influential to all the work I have done in this class as well as work in other courses.

I am gaining a better understanding that there are systematic approaches to teaching reading . . . also learning more about the New York City school system. . . . Having grown up in a very non-diverse, almost all English language speaking town, the environment in the public schools in this city is not something to which I've had a lot of exposure, so I've found it valuable to work closely with those who have more experience in the class.

As these comments reveal, organizing introductory methods courses as a professional community of practice makes visible benefits when differences come together by chance, more likely in public institutions of learning than in those that are private. It also makes visible challenges of an approach that demands support and cooperation, and giving oneself to develop mutually beneficial relationships with unfamiliar others in an institutional setting that imposes other constraints.

Lessons from Teaching to Learn

Emotion and cognition, feeling and thinking combine together in all social practices in complex ways.

Hargreaves (2001, p. 1056)

This retrospective analysis has helped me arrive at new understandings of working toward transformational change in situ. Rereading the writings of course participants and writings that marked significant transitions in my trajectory, I experience a gamut of emotions and vivid recollections of moments of being in a changing emotional landscape. Now with new theoretical tools I am able to do a fresh reading of what escaped me at the time or what I interpreted differently. Specifically I focus on (a) the way participants relate to others in our community of practice and build relationships of trust with the instructor; (b) the level confidence (or uncertainty) that participants convey when talking about their work; and (c) the extent to which they shift from thinking, feeling, and acting like a student to thinking, feeling, and acting like a teacher.

I set out to demonstrate to myself, and to those who joined me on this journey, that it is possible to prepare novices to begin to think, feel, and act like a teacher in a first-semester course organized as a community of practice. The evidence suggests that most, although not all, course participants underwent this transformation. I also organized experiences that challenge preconceptions (and uncertainties) that we all brought to this first-semester course, sometimes intentionally and sometimes unintentionally. Although there is precious little time to devote to making public my thinking on an ongoing basis, many did read my actions as those of a responsive ("caring") educator who wants to help her students to grow. However three individuals from that first memorable semester of 2008 were not reluctant to express their discontent in a manner that I found unusual in comparison with the great majority of critiques that emphasize my "disorganization" because I do not stick to an agenda, or the amount of work I assign.

Two females and one male who shared the same specialization stated that I was "not qualified to teach" and was "unprofessional," and that students learned "next to nothing." Drawing on Lat-Crit theory, I might conclude that my nonmainstream views as a Latinx educator motivated these responses, which may be true, but it is also true that the perspectives I favored did not align with those of their specialization. Lacking knowledge of critiques that colleagues in my program are subjected to, I can only speculate how these unusual comments are worth exploring further for the lessons they embed. In truth, in all my years as faculty, I had never encountered reactions that approximate these three, possibly the result of the new accountability culture that NCLB brought to teacher education. In the next section I elaborate on the challenges I confronted, which provided lessons for similar future efforts.

Challenges of Challenging Preconceptions

As I have described in Chapter 5, teaching is a multifaceted and complex process and a system that stretches across other people and cultural artifacts (Cole & Gajdamaschko, 2007). Learning to teach is also distributed in and across practice settings. This is often a difficult idea to grasp in relation to the view that is pervasive in formal institutional settings across the developmental continuum: that learning depends on the teacher (Britzman, 1999/2003), who must be solely accountable for student performance. However, as I also discovered, some believe that learning in the community is synonymous with letting students teach themselves, in part because this is how I enacted the role of teacher. My planning and orchestrating of activities where I was both participant and observer was not transparent, did not match their expectations, and departed from the instruction of other faculty teaching the same course. Time constraints limit conversations to a few brief comments each week, when some may have benefitted from more in-depth conversations.

Accomplished adults also came to the course with preconceived notions that teaching young children to read in the elementary grades is easy. Some expressed this during initial sessions when I demonstrated the depth of knowledge that is involved in selecting an appropriate book for a read aloud, beginning with the cover illustration of *Rachel*, a "simple" information picture book for third and fourth graders. Regrettably, I did not anticipate having to address these perceptions or misconceptions as the semester began.

Rather than treating knowledge and practice as two distinct aspects of a course that compete for limited time, I integrated knowledge and practice, what Shulman (2005) conceptualizes as pedagogical content knowledge, to support the uptake of practices of high utility in teaching the core content area of English Language Arts, which subsumes reading, writing, speaking, and listening, in low-performing elementary schools. However, as I realized, writing this narrative, emotions also play an important role in bridging the knowledge–practice divide.

One, I drew on my own emotions (more like outrage) and experiences to offer dramatic evidence for what "pedagogically neglected" children are capable of accomplishing in a supportive community of practice when exposed to an intellectually challenging, writing-intensive, inquiry-oriented curriculum that builds on local knowledge. Even after several decades, these writings continue to offer pre- and in-service teachers alternative visions of what is possible, remaining a powerful emotional force in mediating learning for novices learning to teach, as the evidence suggests.

Additionally, teaching a course organized as a community of practice is exhausting work because it requires being a constant presence, monitoring the emotional pulse of accomplished adults who are not used to asking for support, but also to be there for those who are unafraid to seek my assistance. However, few preferred spending more time discussing content as preparation for the content specialty exam because most adults did not anticipate the investment in time that this "simple" methods course required. Some were granted permission to take up the four graduate courses per semester while holding down part-time jobs, adding both tensions and unpredictable vitality to "learning to teach" and "teaching to learn." Some time ago, Winograd and Paris (1988) claimed, and I agree, that literacy is not just a matter of skills or strategies, it is also a matter of will or feelings and emotions. Hargreaves (2001) broadens the range when he argues that all learning occurs within a powerful emotional context that influences how adults engage in teaching–learning encounters in formal practice settings. As I learned through teaching, experiences that heighten tensions and affect engagement included professional readings that discussed alternative perspectives on "literacy," in language that presents unfamiliar assumptions and viewpoints and that is incomprehensible. While some gave themselves to exploring these ideas, resistance on the part of a few was something I was not prepared to address, as Britzman (1999/2003) describes.

The Influence of Institutional Policies and Practices on Learning to Teach

Teacher educators reside in practice settings subject to the influence of institutional policies and practices that shape the courses that we are assigned, the content we are required to include, and the assessment practices we use to measure student competencies in knowledge of content and of teaching, a reality that makes cross-case comparisons of programs difficult. NCLB had a strong presence in my practice setting, shaping my experiences as faculty who brought nonmainstream perspectives to the literacy courses I taught, and where I encountered accomplished adults who may have registered for my sections out of convenience.

However, institutional policies and practices, acting through the power that students are given in specific practice settings, served to delegitimize the professional judgment of experienced faculty who challenged the state policies NCLB generated. In my last semester, I will never forget the moment when someone called out that a required reading I assigned on the developmental pathways of children who experience racism and discrimination in a socially stratified society expressed "racist views" and made "unsubstantiated claims," a comment that left all of us stunned, and I have no recollection of what I said in response. What I do recall is that there was no apparent interest on the part of the individual in exploring the issue in class, and neither did others in the group want to engage in this discussion, and so we moved on. Thinking back on it today, I cannot help associating this comment with the hostile climate NCLB created through politically motivated rhetoric that was dismissive of research that did not meet their narrow criteria of excellence.

Using the lens of Lat-Crit theory made visible moments when ethnicity, culture, and power may have played a role in how participants responded to course content and activities. In truth, I did not find the mistreatment and racist acts that other scholars report (see Ng, Reyes) in my relationship with the adult learners I encountered in the introductory methods course over a three-year period. However, I had experienced it at other times and in other courses, and in my treatment through institutional agents of higher rank. The few comments I acknowledge here are more the exception than the rule, but to leave them out is to render an inaccurate representation of experiences I describe in this narrative.

Conclusion

Two decades ago, Murnane and Levy (1996) argued that schools need to reform both what is being taught and how it is being taught; Zeichner adds schools of education to this group (Zeichner, Payne & Brayko, 2015). As a teaching educator who brought nonmainstream perspectives to a traditional teacher preparation program, I found safety working from the margins, to create a space of radical possibilities, as hooks (1994) describes, to experiment in preparing novices for clinical practice in a college-based first semester course. In that space, from the margin, I was able to mitigate the influence of forces that I did not have the power to control to attain the positive outcomes I value as a community-minded educator. I believe I accomplished this goal with those who trusted me as their guide, and who gave themselves to exploring a way of learning that is less common in institutional settings than it is in real life, and I have reason to believe that many did.

This experience also brought to the forefront issues that we need to attend to as a community of practice. One policy that must be advocated, as a priority, is the preparation of all pre-service teachers/novices with practices of great utility that advance the literacy development of children who live in transnational, multilingual communities, where the number of emergent bilingual children or English language learners in grades one through six is now the majority in the nation's largest cities. For that same reason, the recruitment of faculty who are knowledgeable about biliteracy and biliterate development should be a priority. It is unacceptable that during my tenure I was one of only two full-time faculty with expertise in bilingual and biliterate development in my department.

Edgerton ([1997] 2002) reminds us that "to be a citizen one must not only be informed. One must also care, and be willing to act on one's values and ideas. Central to all the new civic literacies is the development of an emotional identification with the larger community and the belief that, in the face of overwhelming complexity, one individual can make a difference" (p. xx). I trust that the evidence I present in this chapter demonstrates that it is possible to make even a small difference during a brief, four-month semester. And even in the absence of knowing what happened after these accomplished adults completed the course, what I relate on these pages may serve as an inspiration to other teaching educators and to the broader professional community and show that what we do on behalf of the vulnerable children who need our support does matter.

On Reimagining Educator Preparation

I agree with Freire (1998), that living with a commitment to work toward change, and a commitment to live our lives in a manner that embodies our work, helps imbue the spirit of joy in what we do. Because our lives are so deeply intertwined and interconnected with others, it is critical that we listen to one another as we share our stories, our autobiographies, describing and reshaping our Selves as we work to gain deeper understandings of each other (Grumet, 1990) in the interest of those we serve through our work. Maintaining a connection to our individual histories by making them part of our ongoing reflections about teaching, learning, and schools, keeping the broader social context within our gaze, provides us with larger sets of possibilities for our future when reflection leads to critical consciousness and inspires new forms of action.

As pedagogues we are always in conversation with the past in the present. The past informs the present and the present yields lessons that enable us to begin to imagine a better future; in my case as a literacy educator who reimagines a teacher education that is more inclusive of different voices and responsive to the needs of vulnerable children in a world without borders. Writing this professional life history I remember and understand that the path that led me to becoming a teaching educator was born out of human struggle. Benefitting from opportunities created through the sacrifices of others comes with the obligation to continue this work in the present, to create a better future for all children, drawing on the wisdom of diverse communities of practice even as the challenges we confront appear to be insurmountable.

I write to share my experiences and to invite other similar stories from teaching educators from glocal communities near and far, to build much-needed solidarity, to gain a better understanding of how global forces impact local contexts and how local contexts respond in turn. I consider this as a first step toward reinventing teacher preparation in an interdependent world, at a time when new ways to represent meaning and new forms of learning are multiplying, the global migration of families with children is increasing, and the teaching of literacy in childhood education seems seriously out of step with the times (Kress, 1996).

The first part of this chapter summarizes understandings gained from reliving moments in which I tested the boundaries of possibility in educator preparation, with the cooperation of adults who trusted me as their guide. In the second part I reflect on lessons learned from examining the past in the present moment, to begin imagining new possibilities for educator preparation as a global community project that harnesses powerful technological tools to organize informal knowledge-building communities that address our most pressing problems in educator preparation across national borders.

Understandings Gained

Through self-study research I reread interpretations of experiences that remain memorable, and come to new understandings, in the present, of how past experiences inform the present and shape a future we begin to imagine as we read words written long ago.

Disrupting the Teaching Script

From my very first semester as full-time faculty I continued to disrupt the familiar structures of participation in college-based methods courses, disrupting the teaching script that adults have internalized from years of formal schooling, especially post-secondary studies. Activities were writing intensive, and required ongoing (critical) reflection in weekly sessions and as work in progress, as opposed to the passive listening of lectures, note taking, and multiple-choice mid-terms and final exams that were common practice at the time, even in college-based methods courses. I learned a great deal about my well-intentioned practices, especially during those critical first years as an untenured assistant professor, one of two Latinx instructors in the department who taught courses on language development and reading for "bilingual" children (at the time, they were not referred to as English Learners.). Although many came to value learning through the collaborative activities I organized, the session logs completed during the last fifteen minutes of class enabled me to understand how learners' challenges changed over time. In contrast, adult learners in the last three years before my retirement benefitted from what teaching taught me. I was now organizing a similar course, but set out as a community of practice focused on learning to teach core literacy practices that prepare novices to benefit from first clinical experiences in their second semester.

What I failed to realize is that I needed to explain to course participants that they would be entering a new and unfamiliar pedagogical space, which I organized to prepare them to teach the core content area of reading and language arts in the elementary grades (grades one to six), attended primarily by children who live in homes where languages other than English are spoken. Course activities are designed to allow pre- and in-service teachers to develop an understanding of alternative ways to teach and to assess the needs of bilingual or English learners. These activities reflect my studied understanding of instruction as a former classroom teacher in a school where all students were exposed to instruction in English and Spanish. In addition, over a period of three years, I videotaped and studied classroom instruction in schools with high concentrations of children who spoke Spanish and other languages at home, as part of my doctoral research. Therefore, while the activities I organized might appear to be unusual or "strange," they are intended to prepare adults to teach a core content area in local schools that have high concentrations of American children who speak Spanish at home. In effect, pre- and in-service teachers have to understand the character and sources of diversity and the character and sources of appropriate pedagogical responses. For this reason, I needed to monitor carefully the progress that course participants were making as the semester evolved, from what I observed during class sessions and from what they expressed in their reflective writings (initially a session log, completed in the last fifteen minutes of each class and returned with comments).

In truth, my recollection of how I introduced the organization of the session and the class is blurred, which is why I rely on excerpts from session logs to remind me of what we did. Because I have a heightened consciousness that time is fleeting, I can only assume that I offered a brief explanation of how we would work together and then moved on. In retrospect, I should have developed a chart that explained the rules of engagement in "our class," analogous to the ubiquitous "class rules" on display in all elementary school classrooms that I have visited (see Durst (1999) for a similar account of "ground rules" in first-year college composition classes). Another serious problem is that in-service teachers enrolled on at least two courses per semester typically compare activities in courses, and from their analyses I assume that what I did simply did not look like what my colleagues were doing. Out of respect for colleagues and as a new assistant professor, I did not dare to open the topic for discussion during faculty meetings. In retrospect, this difference in approach should not be an individual problem or concern; it is a collective problem or situation that needs to be addressed collaboratively, because there are different ways to enact teaching in college-based clinical practice courses, and as faculty we would want to encourage diversity in approaches to teaching.

A related problem is that the teaching of reading and language arts in the elementary school is the only area of the curriculum that everyone comes in knowing how to teach, or so they think, based on what Lortie (1975) calls the apprenticeship of observation: what they know about teaching having sat in classes as students. Offering new perspectives that change the familiar teaching script is easier said than done. At the very least, faculty in schools of education should engage in conversations to discuss the value of diversifying teaching practice in all college-based clinical practice courses, as a source of strength in teacher preparation.

Institutional Practices and Arrangements

Pre- and in-service teachers, some with part-time jobs, others with full-time jobs, enrolled in at least two courses per semester (sometimes as many as four), typically compared their courses and judged the quality of instruction across different sections of the same or different courses they were either taking or planned to take. Thus comparisons were made on course content, required assignments, and student grading. Under this scrutiny, I was the discrepant case in my department. Although I knew that these comparisons are common, they did not determine the content I considered important or the learning activities that I valued, building on my unique assets and a research base that informed the teaching of reading and language arts to children who live in intergenerational homes, homes where languages other than English are spoken. Thinking about the past in the present, I come to the conclusion that this should not be an individual problem or concern; it is a collective problem or situation that needs to be addressed departmentally, because there are different ways to enact teaching in college-based clinical practice. In the same way we benefit from student diversity, we also benefit from pedagogical diversity.

Learning to Teach from Those I Teach

That we learn from our students is to be expected because students always teach us in the smallest, day-to-day moments. However, there are times when what we learn from our students has a major impact on our actions and our thinking as pedagogues, in effect, reorienting us to the world. I had one of those moments over twenty years ago, when a lovely young woman with Asian features registered for two of my classes: the reading methods course in 1993 and an independent study on research and evaluation in the spring of 1994. I do not recall precisely when Cecile Chong spoke to me in flawless Spanish, possibly during a session of the reading course that I refer to as the Spanish immersion experience, when I switch to speaking only Spanish for about twenty minutes. Curious as to where she learned Spanish, Cecile explained to me that she is of Chinese ancestry and was born and schooled in Ecuador.

Since that day, the Asian diversity in Latin America has been a subject that has intrigued me, compelling engagement in historical research that has led to tracing its origins to the European colonization of the Americas, beginning with Columbus's explorations on behalf of the Spanish monarchy, and the beginnings of what we now refer to as globalization. As someone who enjoys eating at Cuban-Chinese restaurants I did not think to question the origins of the tasty Cuban-Chinese food that I love. However, in an educational setting, learning about Cecile's experience had a different significance, and brought attention to what might have remained unknown. Cecile does not know that I added two children's books by a Guatemalan author of Chinese ancestry to my collection (*Sawdust Carpets* and *Mommy and Daddy Have a Store* by Amelia Lau Carling) because of what I learned from her. I raise this point because in teacher education we emphasize that the teachers need to know their students in order to teach, well-intentioned advice that sometimes leads to stereotypic thinking about diversity given that what is accessible online often misrepresents cultural information. I learned about Cecile's background out of curiosity as to how she learned Spanish. With young children it may be preferable to use a children's book that creates spaces to learn about the background of our students indirectly, by allowing them to respond to the words and images that appear in quality children's books by authors who are knowledgeable about the subject.

I learned from teaching through the power of the printed word, in time and across time. As I illustrate in Chapter 4, session logs and other embedded writings that we discuss in class generate data that yield insights into the learning experiences that shape our transactions, specifically about the content load of the course, mostly required readings and assignments, which I act on with immediacy. Examining these writings over time with a different set of theoretical lenses I detect new patterns in familiar data that make visible robust findings.

On a final note, I should like to reiterate that these understandings also have policy implications for college-based teacher education programs, and the state agencies that issue educational policies that taxpayer dollars support. I have come to understand that we have the responsibility to make these lived experiences public, because those who sponsor and support public education have a right to know that the sources of educational problems reported in the press are often the result of hastily and politically motivated policy by high-level management, which school administrators and educators are obligated to follow.

Reimagining Educator Preparation as a Global Enterprise

In this section, I draw on a forty-year trajectory, the movement to reinvent teacher preparation that is shaped by the needs of local communities and builds on the experiences of families, children, and youth. Reimagining educator preparation as a global enterprise begins by harnessing the power of information and technological tools, and human and material resources from global professional communities of practice to develop and strengthen formal and informal knowledge-building communities in a borderless world.

Diversity as a Source of Strength in Educator Preparation

Learning from others who have backgrounds and characteristics very different from our own is a source of strength in educator preparation, and in the teaching–learning process across the developmental continuum (Sleeter, 2001; Cochran-Smith & Villegas, 2015). I found this need for intersubjectivity to be true as a college-based teaching educator who was, at one time, one of five full-time Latinx faculty members in my department. As data generated from teaching documents, the cultural, linguistic, and experiential capital that I brought to teaching was valued by the majority of pre-and in-service teachers I encountered in my classes, in the same way that I valued the different experiences and backgrounds of the adults that entered my pedagogical space by chance, each semester. Studies of diversity in university settings conclude that diversity enhances the teaching and learning process in higher education, adding that, "in an increasingly diverse country that is inextricably connected to a larger 'global' community, we must reconsider what it means to be an active and productive member of society" (Milem, 2003, chapter 5, p. 1).

Yet, despite the social and intellectual benefits that result from diversity, it is concerning that the diversity that exists on "campus" (the four buildings that comprised the college) is not to be found in our teacher preparation programs, increasingly during the last decade of my tenure. It is shocking to consider that in a city where the world resides, and that is present in our public schools, the teaching staff is over 80 percent Caucasian. This is not a new problem, but I can say with certainty that there was far more diversity in my early years of teaching children and adults than there is presently; a diversity that resulted from global social movements. Although most explanations of the limited presence of cultural and linguistic diversity in college-based teacher education attribute it to racism, a few emphasize that the teaching professions are no longer held in high esteem, or that they simply did not pay as well as other professions for the same level of preparation. There is truth in all of these explanations. Nevertheless, the minimal cultural and linguistic diversity that is found in the teaching staff of the nation's largest school district is a problem not just for adults, but especially for the young, who seldom encounter others who look like them and serve as role models and mentors and likely to lessen the social distance between first-year teachers and children they will encounter in the under-resourced schools where they will be placed.

Connecting Communities of Practice on a Global Scale

Blurring the boundaries between the school, the home, and college-based teacher preparation in which I worked side-by-side with children, their families, their teachers, and colleagues has taught me that collaborating in communities of practice is a potent force in challenging institutional policies and practices that serve neither our children, nor our society well, while building the self-esteem and confidence of children and youth that are not well served by schools. Writing about these experiences heightens consciousness of the power of connecting diverse communities of practice, including the role that my experiences and background played in the process. These experiences include but are not limited to cultural values and beliefs that define and sustain me in challenging times, and a bilingualism and biliteracy that allow me to navigate many different social worlds and cultural milieus, seeking to learn from others and other ways of being a teaching educator, and organizing teacher preparation as the world grows smaller and more complex. The lived experiences that I share on the pages of this book are precisely how I reimagine the preparation of teachers in a world without borders. I begin by examining the challenges I confronted during my forty-year trajectory as an educator.

Confronting Inequality in Teacher Education

I reimagine educator preparation as I confront inequality, and am forced to ponder: What new challenges need attention? How could things be otherwise? As I have learned from lived experience, working toward change is not possible without the collaboration of others, or other communities of practice that inform and contribute to educator preparation, e.g., public schools, families, local communities, institutions of higher education. Our challenge is to build connections within and across national boundaries, inherently complex and challenging work. As Cochran-Smith (2004) suggests, this work involves the negotiation of conflicting values about the purposes, roles, and content of schooling at a time when teacher education is under the influence of power brokers that are succeeding in privatizing public education, promoting curriculum uniformity and faculty accountability as a global project (Stromquist & Monkman, 2014). This is exemplified by the Global Education Reform Movement (or GERM) and the Teach for All approach to educator preparation, which, guided by a vision that seeks to limit government intervention in our lives, are methodically eroding confidence in public education and undermining the social and civic mission of public education. Even so, unexpected opportunities created by powerful technological tools enable access to information and resources that may be used to organize new knowledge-building communities that are responsive to glocal educational needs across national borders, with assistance from professional organizations such as the World Education Research Association (WERA). Through its annual gatherings in major cities around the world, WERA creates spaces to meet with and learn from colleagues who share common concerns. These efforts create new possibilities and opportunities to build much needed solidarity across national borders.

Insights gained from writing this professional life history as a community-oriented educator suggest that it is possible to begin working for change in the unofficial, in-between spaces through collaboration with professionals who work on behalf of vulnerable children, families, and communities. It appeared natural to me that in my first year of teaching as full-time faculty, I engaged three critical communities of practice that affect school learning—the schools that children attend, the homes and communities where they live, and the college-based courses where we prepare teachers to teach children from these communities. Developing these relationships, and inhabiting each other's spaces happened because we shared a similar vision and the will to engage. Subsequently, we engaged with other professional communities that inform education and teacher preparation—

professional organizations where students, teachers, and teacher educators assumed a new role. Despite the hard work that working for change requires, I found joy in working for and experimenting with alternative ways to enact teacher preparation, as Freire (1998) describes. Today, long after some of these communities have ceased to exist, the power of the printed word preserves them in time and place, and also transports them to other parts of the world. This is why all teaching educators who are similarly engaged need to write their professional life histories as a way to build much needed solidarity in these complex times.

Bibliography

Adamson, F., Astrand, B. & L. Darling Hammond (2016). *Global education reform: How privatization and public investment influence education outcomes*. New York: Routledge.

Anderson, A.B. & S.J. Stokes (1984). Social and institutional influences on the development and practice of literacy (pp. 24–37). In H. Goelman, A. Oberg, and F. Smith (Eds.), *Awakening to literacy*. Exeter, NH: Heinemann.

Anyon, J. (Winter, 1980). Social class and the hidden curriculum of work. *The Journal of Education*, 1(1), 67–92.

Apple, M. (2011). Global crisis, social justice and teacher education. *Journal of Teacher Education*, 62(2), 222–234.

Armbruster, B.B., F. Lehr & J. Osborn (2003). *Put reading first: The research building blocks for teaching children to read: Kindergarten through grade*, 2nd edn. CIERA. Available online: https://www.nichd.nih.gov/publications/product/239; Download the most recent version at: https://lincs.ed.gov/publications/pdf/ PRFbooklet.pdf

Armstrong, C.P., E.M. Achilles & M.J. Sacks (1935). Report of the Special Commission on Immigration and Naturalization of the Chamber of Commerce of the State of New York, "Reactions of Puerto Rican Children in New York to Psychological Tests."

Ashton-Warner, S. (1963). *Teacher*. New York, NY: Bantam Books.

Au, K.H. (1993). *Literacy instruction in multicultural settings*. New York, NY: Harcourt, Brace Jovanovich.

Au, K.H. & C. Jordan (1981). Teaching reading to Hawaiian children: Finding a culturally appropriate solution (pp. 139–152). In H.T. Trueba, G.P. Guthrie, and K.H. Au (Eds.), *Culture and the bilingual classroom*. Rowley, MA: Newbury House Publishers.

August, D. & K. Hakuta (Eds.) (1997). *Schooling for language minority schooling: A research agenda*. Washington, DC: National Academy Press.

August, D. & T. Shanahan (Eds.) (2006). *Developing literacy in second language learners: Report of the national literacy panel on language-minority children and youth*. Mahwah, NJ: Lawrence Erlbaum.

Ball, D.L. (2010). Summary of Testimony to U.S. House of Representatives Committee on Education and Labor.

Ball, D.L. & F.M. Forzani (2011). Building a common core for learning to teach, and connecting professional learning to practice. *American Educator*, 35(2), 17–21, 38–39.

Ballenger, C. (1999). *Teaching other people's children: Literacy and learning in a bilingual classroom*. New York, NY: Teachers College Press.

Banks, J.A. (1998). The lives and values of researchers: Implications for educating citizens in a multicultural society. *Educational Researcher*, 27(7), 4–17.

Banks, J. et al. (2007). Learning in and out of school: Life-long, life-wide, life-deep. The LIFE Center and the Center for Multicultural Education at the University of Washington. Available online: http://www.life-slc.org/ (accessed October 10, 2007).

Barnes, M.E. & P. Smagorinsky (2016). What English/Language Arts teacher candidates learn during coursework and practica: A study of three teacher education programs. *Journal of Teacher Education*, 67(4), 338–355. Available online: http://www.petersmagorinsky.net/About/PDF/JTE/JTE2016.pdf

Barrera, R. (1981). Reading in Spanish: Insights from children's miscue analysis. In S. Hudelson (Ed.), *Learning to read in different languages*. Arlington, VA: Center for Applied Linguistics.

Barton, D. & M. Hamilton (1998). *Local literacies: Reading and writing in one community*. London: Routledge.

Beck, I. & M.G. McKeown (2001). Text Talk: Capturing the benefits of read aloud experiences for young children. *The Reading Teacher*, 55(1), 10–20.

Berchini, C. (2016). Curriculum matters: The Common Core, authors of color, and inclusion for inclusion's sake. *Journal of Adolescent & Adult Literacy*, 60(1), 55–62.

Berchini, C. (December, 2017). "But the kids can't handle that!": Disrupting the deep structures and ideologies of educational institutions for equity & inclusion. Invited address for the faculty and students of the Neag School of Education, University of Connecticut, Storrs.

Berliner, D. (2009). *Poverty and potential: Out-of-School factors and school success*. Boulder and Tempe: Education and the Public Interest Center & Education Policy Research.

Berliner, D.C. (2014a). Exogenous variables and value-added assessments: A fatal flaw. *Teachers College Record*, 116(1). Available online: http://www.tcrecord.org/content.asp?contentid=17293 (accessed July 21, 2014).

Berliner, D. (2014b). Inequality, poverty and the widening education gap. *Teachers College Record*, 116(1), 1. Available online: http://www.tcrecord.org, ID Number: 16889 (accessed October 17, 2012).

Bernhardt, E.B. (1991/1998). *Reading development in a second language: Theoretical, empirical, & classroom perspectives*. Norwood, NJ: Ablex Publishing.

Board of Education of the City of New York (1958). The Puerto Rican Study, 1953–1957. A report on the education and adjustment of Puerto Rican pupils in the public schools in the City of New York.

Board of Education of the City of New York (1967/1968). A guide for beginning teachers. *Curriculum Bulletin*, 1967–68 Series.

Bravo, M., E. Hiebert & D. Pearson (2007). Tapping the linguistic resources of Spanish/English bilinguals: The role of cognates in science (pp. 140–156). In R.K. Wagner,

A. Muse, and K. Tannenbaum (Eds.), *Vocabulary development and its implications for reading comprehension*. New York, NY: Guilford.

Brittain, C. (2009). Transnational messages: What teachers can learn from understanding students' lives in transnational social spaces. *The High School Journal*, 92(4), 100–113.

Britzman, D.P. (2000). Teacher education in the confusion of our times. *Journal of Teacher Education*, 51, 200–205.

Britzman, D.P. (2003). *Practice makes practice: A critical study of learning to teach*, 2nd edn. Albany, NY: State University of New York Press.

Britzman, D.P. (2009). Teacher education as uneven development: Toward a psychology of uncertainty. In A. Pitts (Ed.), *Keynotes in teacher education: CATE Invited Addresses 2004–2008* vol. 1. Ottawa, Canada: Canadian Association for Teacher Education.

Britzman, D.P. (2013). Between psychoanalysis and pedagogy: Scenes of rapprochement and alienation. *Curriculum Inquiry*, 43(1), 95–117.

Bronfenbrenner, U. (1979). *The ecology of human development*. Cambridge, MA: Harvard University Press.

Brookline Teacher Researcher Seminar (2003). *Regarding children's words: Teacher research on language and literacy*. New York: Teachers College Press.

Brown, J.S., A. Collins & P. Duguid (1989). Situated cognition and the culture of learning. *Educational Researcher*, 18(1), 32–42.

Bruner, J. (1986). *Actual minds, possible worlds*. Cambridge, MA: Harvard University Press.

Bruner, J. (1996). *The culture of education*. Cambridge, MA: Harvard University Press.

Calderhead, J. (2001). International experiences of teaching reform (pp. 77–800). In V. Richardson (Ed.), *Handbook of research on teaching*, 4th edn. Washington, DC: AERA.

Carrasco, R.L., A. Vera & C. Cazden (1981). Aspects of bilingual students' communicative competence in the classroom: A case study. In R.P. Duran (Ed.), *Latino language and communicative behavior*. Norwood, NJ: Ablex.

Carter, K. (1993). The place of story in the study of teaching and teacher education. *Educational Researcher*, 22(1), 5–12.

Carter, K. & W. Doyle (1996). Personal narrative and life history in learning to teach (pp. 120–142). In J. Sikula, T.J. Buttery, and E. Guyton (Eds.), *Handbook of research on teacher education*, 2nd edn. New York, NY: Macmillan.

Cazden, C. (1980). Culturally responsive education: Recommendations for achieving the Lau Remedies (pp. 69–86). In H.T. Trueba, G.P. Guthrie, and K.H. Au (Eds.), *Culture and the bilingual classroom*. Rowley, MA: Newbury House Publishers.

Cazden, C. (1988). *Classroom discourse: The language of teaching and learning*. Portsmouth, NH: Heinemann.

Chall, J. & V. Jacobs (2003). Poor children's fourth-grade slump. *American Educator*, 27(1), 14–15.

Chall, J.S., V.A. Jacobs & I.E. Baldwin (1990). *The reading crisis: Why poor children fall behind.* Cambridge, MA: Harvard University Press.

Chamot, A.U. & J.M. O'Malley (1994). *The CALLA handbook: Implementing the cognitive, academic language approach.* Reading, MA: Addison-Wesley Publishing Company (chapter 5, pp. 83–101).

Chartier, R. (1995). *Forms and meanings.* Philadelphia, PA: University of Pennsylvania Press.

Chase, S.E. (2005). Narrative inquiry: Multiple lenses, approaches, voices (pp. 651–679). In N.K. Denzin and Y.S. Lincoln (Eds.), *The Sage handbook of qualitative research,* 3rd edn. London, Thousand Oaks, CA, and New Delhi: Sage.

Clift, R.T. & P. Brady (2005). Research on methods courses and field experiences (pp. 261–308). In M. Cochran-Smith and K.M. Zeichner (Eds.), *Studying teacher education: The report of the AERA Panel on research and teacher education.* Washington, DC: The American Education Research Association.

Coballes-Vega, C., C. Espino-Paris & A.F. Marra (1979). The Title VII (Bilingual) Fellowship Program: A Preliminary Report, April 1979. Bilingual Education Paper Series, vol. 2, no. 9. National Evaluation and Assessment Center: California State University, Los Angeles. ED 230 346.

Cochran-Smith, M. (1995). Uncertain allies: Understanding the boundaries of race and teaching. *Harvard Educational Review,* 65(4), 541–571.

Cochran-Smith, M. (2004). *Walking the road: Race, diversity, and social justice in teacher education.* New York, NY: Teachers College Press.

Cochran-Smith, M. & A.M. Villegas (2015). Framing teacher preparation research: An overview of the field, part 1. *Journal of Teacher Education,* 66(1), 7–20.

Cochran-Smith, M. & K.M. Zeichner (Eds.) (2005). *Studying teacher education: The report of the AERA Panel on research and teacher education.* Washington, DC: The American Education Research Association.

Cole, M. & N. Gajdamaschko (2007). Vygotsky and culture (pp. 193–211). In H. Daniels, M. Cole, and J.V. Wertsch (Eds.), *The Cambridge companion to Vygotsky.* New York, NY: Cambridge University Press.

Collins, C. (2011). *"Ethnically qualified": Race, merit, and the selection of urban teachers, 1920–1980.* New York, NY: Teachers College Press.

Comer, J.P., Chair (2006). Child and adolescent development research and teacher education: Evidence-based pedagogy, policy, and practice. Summary of roundtable meetings, December 1–2, 2005 and March 20–21, 2006. Co-sponsored by the National Institute of Child Health and Human Development (NICHD) & the National Council for Accreditation of Teacher Education (NCATE).

Cordasco, F. & F.P. Sanjek (1969). a. *Peabody Journal of Education,* 47(3), 160–163.

Council of Chief State School Officers (2011). *InTASC model core teaching standards: A resource for state dialogue.* Washington, DC: Council of Chief State School Officers.

Cummins, J. (1981). Interdependency of first and second language proficiency in bilingual children (pp. 70–89). In E. Bialystock (Ed.), *Language processing in bilingual children*. Cambridge: Cambridge University Press.

Dall'Alba, G. & R. Barnacle (2007). An ontological turn for higher education. *Studies in Higher Education*, 32(6), 679–691.

Dalton, S.S. (1998). Pedagogy matters: Standards for effective teaching practice. Research report no. 4. Center for Research on Education, Diversity and Excellence.

Daniels, H. (2007). Pedagogy (pp. 307–331). In H. Daniels, M. Cole, and J.V. Wertsch (Eds.), *The Cambridge companion to Vygotsky*. Cambridge, MA: Cambridge University Press.

Darling-Hammond, L. (1998). Teachers and teaching: Testing policy hypotheses from a national commission report. *Educational Researcher*, 27(1), 5–15.

Darling-Hammond, L. & J. Bransford (Eds.) (2005). *Preparing teachers for a changing world: What teachers should learn and be able to do*. Sponsored by the National Academy of Education. San Francisco, CA: John Wiley & Sons.

Delgado Bernal, D. (2008). *La trenza de identidades*: Weaving together my personal, professional, and communal identities (pp. 135–148). In K.P. González and R.V. Padilla (Eds.), *Doing the public good: Latina/o scholars engage in civic participation*. Sterling, VA: Stylus.

DeNicolo, C.P. & M.E. Franquiz (2006). "Do I have to say it?" Critical encounters with multicultural children's literature. *Language Arts*, 84(2), 157–170.

Development & Dissemination Project (1999). A 4-year initiative between the Education Alliance at Brown University and the Office of Bilingual Education of the New York City Board of Education under the leadership of Dr. Lillian Hernandez (1998–2002).

Dewey, J. (1916). *Democracy and education. An introduction to the philosophy of education*. New York, NY: Macmillan.

Dewey, J. (1938). *Experience and education*. New York, NY: Macmillan.

Diaz, S., L.C. Moll & H. Mehan (1986). Sociocultural resources for instruction: A context-specific approach (pp. 187–230). In *Beyond language: Social and cultural factors in schooling language minority students*. Compiled by the California State Board of Education, Los Angeles: Bilingual Education Office: Evaluation, Dissemination and Assessment Center.

Dickson, S.V., D.C. Simmons & E.J. Kameenui (1998). Text organization: Instructional & curricular bases and implications (chapter 11). In D.C. Simmons and E. Kameenui (Eds.), *What reading research tells us about children with diverse learning needs: Bases and basics*. Mahwah, NJ: Lawrence Erlbaum Associates.

Donaldson, M. (1978). *Children's minds*. London: Fontana/Croom Helm.

Doyle, W. & K. Carter (2003). Narrative and learning to teach: Implications for teacher education curriculum. *Journal of Curriculum Studies*, 35(2), 129–137.

Du Bois, W.E.B. (1903). *The souls of black folk: Essays and sketches*. Chicago, IL: A.C. McClurg & Co.

Duckworth, E. (1986). Teaching as research. *Harvard Educational Review*, 56, 481–495.

Duderstadt, J. (2008). *Aligning American higher education with a 21st century public agenda*. Miller Center of Public Affairs. Association of governing boards.

Duncan, A. (November, 2010). The new normal: Doing more with less—Secretary Arnie Duncan's remarks at the American Enterprise Institute (downloaded from ED. Gov., U.S. Dept. of Education).

Duranti, A. & E. Ochs (1996). Syncretic literacy: Multiculturalism in Somoan American families. Available online: https://www.ncela.gwu.edu/miscpubs/ncrdsll/rr16/index.htm

Durgunoglu, A.Y. & L. Verhoeven (Eds.) (1998). *Literacy development in multilingual contexts: Cross cultural perspectives*. Mahwah, NJ: Lawrence Erlbaum Associates.

Durst, R.K. (1999). *Collision course: Conflict, negotiation and learning in college composition*. Urbana, IL: National Council on the Teaching of English. Available online: https://files.eric.ed.gov/fulltext/ED427340.pdf (accessed January 13, 2018).

Dyson, A.H. (1993). From prop to mediator: The changing role of written language in children's symbolic repertoire (pp. 21–41). In B. Spodek and O.N. Saracho (Eds.), *Language and literacy in early childhood education*. New York, NY: Teachers College Press.

Edelsky, C. (1983). *Writing in a bilingual program: Habia una vez*. Norwood, NJ: Ablex.

Edgerton, R. ([1997] 2001). Higher Education White Paper. Pew Charitable Trusts.

Educational Commission of the States (ECS), December 2013, vol. 14, no 6. English Language Learners.

Entwisle, D.R. & K.L. Alexander (1993). Entry into school: The beginning school transition and educational stratification in the United States. *Annual Review of Sociology*, 19, 401–423.

Epstein, J.L. (1995). School, family and community partnerships. *Phi Delta Kappan*, 76(9), 701–711.

Finn, C.E. (2004). The original education president: Reagan's ABCs. *National Review*, June 9. Available online: http://www.nationalreview.com/article/211015/original-education-president-chester-e-finn-jr

Flores, B.M. (1990). Children's psychogenesis of literacy and biliteracy (pp. 281–320). In *Proceedings of the first research symposium on limited English proficient students' issues*. Washington, DC: Office of Bilingual Education and Minority Language Affairs, U.S. Department of Education and Minority Language Affairs.

Florio-Ruane, S. (2002). An argument for complexity in studies of teacher education. *Journal of Teacher Education*, 53(3), 205–215.

Foot, K.A. (2014). Cultural-Historical Activity Theory: Exploring a theory to inform practice. *Journal of Human Behavior in the Social Environment*, 4(3), 329–347.

For Each and Every Child: A strategy for education excellence and equity. Released February 2013. Available online: http://www.civilrights.org/publications/reports/education-equity-report/the-equity-and-excellence.html (accessed May 16, 2017).

Forzani, F.M. (2014). Understanding core practices and practice-based teacher education: Learning from the past. *Journal of Teacher Education*, 65(4), 357–368.

Freebody, P. & A. Luke (1990). Literacies programs: Debates and demands in cultural context. *Prospect: An Australian Journal of TESOL*, 5(3), 7–16.

Freire, P. (1998). *Pedagogy of freedom: Ethics, democracy and civic courage.* Lanham, MD: Rowman & Littlefield Publishers.

Gadotti, M. (1996). *Pedagogy of praxis.* Albany, NY: SUNY Press.

Garcia Coll, C. & L.A. Szalacha (1996). An integrative model for the study of developmental competencies in minority children. *Child Development*, 67(5), 1891–1914.

Garrison, J. & A. Neiman (2003). Pragmatism and education (pp. 21–37). In N. Blake, P. Smeyers, R. Smith, and P. Standish (Eds.), *The Blackwell guide to the philosophy of education.* Malden, MA: Blackwell Publishing.

Gautreaux, M. & S. Delgado (2016). Portrait of a Teach for All (TfA) teacher: Media narratives of the universal TfA teacher in 12 countries. *Education Policy Analysis Archives*, 24(110). Available online: http://dx.doi.org/10.14507/epaa.24.2149

Gay, G. (2010). *Culturally responsive teaching: Theory, research, and practice*, 2nd edn. New York, NY: Teachers College Press.

Goelman, H., A. Oberg & F. Smith (Eds.) (1984). *Awakening to literacy.* Exeter, NH: Heinemann.

Goldenberg, C. (Summer, 2008). Teaching English Language Learners. What the research says and does not say. *American Educator*, 8–44. Available online: https://www.aft.org/sites/default/files/periodicals/goldenberg.pdf

Goldman, S.R. & J. Wiley (2004). Discourse analysis: Written text (pp. 62–91). In N.K. Duke and M.H. Mallette (Eds.), *Literacy research methodologies.* New York: The Guilford Press.

Gonzalez, N., L.C. Moll & C. Amanti (2005). *Funds of knowledge: Theorizing practices in households, communities and classrooms.* Mahwah, NJ: Lawrence Erlbaum Associates.

Goodwin, A.L., L. Smith, M. Souto-Manning, R. Cheruvu, M.Y. Tan, R. Reed & L. Taveras (2014). What should teacher educators know and be able to do? Perspectives from practicing teachers. *Journal of Teacher Education*, 65(4), 284–302.

Goody, J. (2000). *The power of the written tradition.* Washington, DC: Smithsonian Institution Press.

Greaney, V. (Ed.). (1996). *Promoting reading in developing countries.* Newark, DE: International Reading Association.

Greene, M. (1978). Teaching: The question of personal reality. *Teachers College Record*, 80(1), 23–35.

Greene, M. (1993). The passions of pluralism: Multiculturalism and the expanding community. *Educational Researcher*, 22(1), 13–18.

Greene, M. (2001). Defining aesthetic education (pp. 5–6). In *Variations on a blue guitar.* The Lincoln Center Institute in Aesthetic Education.

Grossman, P. (2005). Pedagogical approaches in teacher education (pp. 425–476). In M. Cochran-Smith and K. Zeichner (Eds.), *Studying teacher education: A report of the AERA panel on research and teacher education.* Mahwah, NJ: Lawrence Erlbaum Associates.

Grumet, M. (1990). Retrospective: Autobiography and the analysis of educational experience. *Cambridge Journal of Education*, 20(3), 321–325.

Grumet, M. (2010). The public expression of citizen teachers. *Journal of Teacher Education*, 61(1/2), 66–76.

Gudmundsdottir, S. (2001). Narrative research on school practice (pp. 226–240). In V. Richardson (Ed.), *Handbook of research on teaching*, 4th edn. Washington, DC: AERA.

Haberman, M. (1991). The pedagogy of poverty versus good teaching. *Phi Delta Kappan*, 73(4), 290–294.

Haberman, M. (2000). What makes a teacher education program relevant preparation for teaching diverse students in urban poverty schools? (The Milwaukee Teacher Education Center Model).

Haberman, M. (2005). *Star Teachers: The ideology of best practice of effective teachers of diverse children and youth in poverty*. Houston, TX: Haberman Educational Foundation.

Hades, D. (1997). Reading multiculturally (pp. 233–275). In V. Harris (Ed.), *Using multiethnic literature in the K-8 classroom*. Norwood, MA: Christopher-Gordon Publishers.

Haidt, J. (2012). *The righteous mind: Why good people are divided by politics and religion*. New York, NY: Vintage.

Hammerness, K., L. Darling-Hammond, J. Bransford with D. Berliner, M. Cochran-Smith, M. McDonald & K. Zeichner (2005). How teachers learn and develop (pp. 358–389). In L. Darling-Hammond and J. Bransford (Eds.), *Preparing teachers for a changing world*. Sponsored by the National Academy of Education. San Francisco, CA: John Wiley & Sons.

Hamre, B.K. & R.C. Pianta (2005). Can instructional and emotional support in the first grade classroom make a difference for children at risk of school failure? *Child Development*, 76(5), 949–967.

Hargreaves, A. (2001). Emotional geographies of teaching. *Teachers College Press*, 103(16), 1056–1080.

Hartse, H.C., V. Woodward & C.I. Burke (1984). *Language stories and literacy lesson*. Portsmouth, NH: Heinemann.

Heath, S.B. (1983). *Ways with words*. New York, NY: Cambridge University Press.

Heath, S.B. (1985). Literacy or literate skills? Considerations for ESL/EFL learners (pp. 15–28). In P. Larson, E.L. Judd, and L.S. Messerschmidt (Eds.), *On TESOL '84: Brave new world for TESOL*. Washington, DC: TESOL.

Hiebert, E. & C. Fischer (May, 2005). A review of the national reading panel's studies on fluency: The role of text. *The Elementary School Journal*, 105(5), 443–460.

Hirsch, E.D. (2003). Reading comprehension requires knowledge—of words and the world. *American Educator*, 27(1), 10–13, 16–22, 28–29.

Holdaway, D. (1979). *The foundations of literacy*. Gosford, NSW: Scholastic Press.

Holdaway, D. (1982). Shared book experience: Teaching reading using favorite books. *Theory into Practice*, 21(4), 293–300.

Hudelson, S. (1984). *Kan u ret and rayt en ingles*: Children become literate in English as a second language. *TESOL Quarterly*, 18, 221–238.

Hudelson, S. (1986). ESL children's writing: What we've learned, what we're learning (pp. 23–54). In P. Rigg and D. S. Enright (Eds.), *Children and ESL: Integrating perspectives*. Washington, DC: Teaching English to Speakers of Other Languages.

Huerta, T.M. & C.M. Brittain (2010). Effective practices that matter for Latino children. In E.G. Murrillo, Jr. (Ed.), *Handbook of Latinos in Education*. New York, NY: Routledge.

hooks, b. (1994). *Teaching to transgress*. New York, NY: Routledge.

Keats, E.J. (1981). *Regards to the man in the moon*. New York, NY: Viking.

Kellner, D. (2000). Globalization and new social movements: Lessons for critical theory and pedagogy (pp. 299–321). In N.C. Burbules and C.A. Torres (Eds.), *Globalization and education: Critical perspectives*. New York, NY: Routledge.

Kemmis, S. (March, 2010). Research for praxis: Knowing doing. *Pedagogy, Culture & Society*, 8(1), 9–27.

Knobel, M. (1999). *Everyday literacies: Students, discourse and social practice*. New York, NY: Peter Lang.

Kozol, J. (1992). *Savage inequalities: Children in America's schools*. New York, NY: Perennial.

Kress, G. (1996). Internationalization and globalization: Rethinking a curriculum of communication. *Comparative Education*, 32(2), Special no. 18: Comparative Education and Post-Modernity, 185–196.

Kucsera, J. & G. Orfield (March 2014). New York State's extreme school segregation: Inequality, inaction and a damaged future. The Civil Rights Project.

LaBoskey, V.K. (2004). The methodology of self-study and its theoretical underpinnings (pp. 817–869). In J.J. Loughran et al. (Eds.), *International handbook of self-study of teaching and teacher education practices*. New York, NY: Springer International Handbooks of Education, volume 12.

Labov, W. (1972). *Language in the inner city*. Philadelphia, PA: University of Pennsylvania Press.

Labov, W. (1987). The community as educator (pp. 128–146). In J. Langer (Ed.), *Language literacy and culture: Issues of society and schooling*. Norwood, NJ: Ablex.

Ladson-Billings, G. (1994). *The dreamkeepers*. San Francisco, CA: Jossey-Bass.

Ladson-Billings, G.J. (2005). Is the team all right? Diversity in teacher education. *Journal of Teacher Education*, 56(3), 229–234.

Lampert, M. (2010). Learning teaching in, from and of practice: What do we mean? *Journal of Teacher Education*, 61(1), 21–34.

Lampert, M. & F. Graziani (2009). Instructional activities as a tool for teachers' and teacher educators' learning. *The Elementary School Journal*, 109(5), 491–509.

Lampert, M., M.L. Franke, E. Kazemi, H. Ghousseini, A.C. Turrou, H. Beasely, A. Cunard & K. Crowe (2013). Keeping it complex: Using rehearsals to support novice teachers' learning of ambitious teaching. *Journal of Teacher Education*, 64(3), 226–243.

Latina Feminist Group, The (2001). *Telling to live: Latina feminist testimonios.* Durham, NC: Duke University Press.

Lave, J. (1996). Teaching, as learning, in practice. *Mind, Culture and Activity,* 3(3), 149–164.

Lave, J. & E. Wenger (1991). *Situated learning.* New York: Cambridge University Press.

Levine, A. (2009). Waiting for the transformation. *Education Week,* February 5, 2009. Available online: http://www.edweek.org/ew/articles/2009/02/25levine_ep.h28. html?tmp=724029534J (accessed April 10, 2018).

Lortie, D. (1975). *Schoolteacher: A sociological study.* Chicago, IL: University of Chicago Press.

Loughran, J. (1997). Teaching about teaching: Principles and practice (pp. 57–69). In T. Russell and J. Loughran (Eds.), *Teaching about teaching: Purpose, passion and pedagogy in teacher education.* Bristol, PA: Falmer Press & Taylor and Francis.

Loughran, J. (2005). *Developing a pedagogy of teacher education: Understanding teaching and learning about teaching.* New York, NY: Routledge.

Loughran, J. (2007). Enacting a pedagogy of teacher education (pp. 1–15). In T. Russell and J. Loughran (Eds.), *Enacting a pedagogy of teacher education: Values, relationships and practices.* New York, NY: Routledge.

Luke, A. (2004). Teaching after the market: From commodity to cosmopolitan. *Teachers College Record,* 106(7), 1422–1443.

Luke, A. (2012). Critical literacy: Foundational notes. *Theory into Practice,* 51(1), 4–11.

Luke, A., A. Woods & K. Dooley (2011). Comprehension as social and intellectual practice: Rebuilding curriculum in low socioeconomic and cultural minority schools. *Theory into Practice,* 50, 157–164.

Machado, A.M. ([1995]2001). *Nina Bonita.* E. Iribarren (trans.), R. Faria (illus.). La Jolla, CA: Kane/Miller Book Publishers.

Machado, A.M. ([1982]2002). *Me in the middle [Bisa Bia, Bisa Bel].* D. Unger (trans.), C. Merola (illus.). Toronto: Groundwood Books.

Machado, A.M. ([2002]2005). *From another world.* Sao Paulo, Brazil: Editora Atica.

Mangual, A. (1996). *A history of reading.* New York, NY: The Pen.

Margolies, R.J. (May, 1968). *The losers: A report on Puerto Ricans in the public schools.* Commissioned by Aspira of New York. ED 023 779.

Martínez-Roldán, C.M. (2013). The representation of Latinos and the use of Spanish: A critical content analysis of Skippyjon Jones. *Journal of Children's Literature,* 39(1), 5–14.

McCagg, W.O. (1989). The origins of defectology (pp. 39–62). In W.O. McCagg and L. Siegelbaum (Eds.), *The disabled in the Soviet Union: Past and present, theory and practice.* Pittsburgh, PA: University of Pittsburgh Press.

McCarty, T.L. (Ed) (2005). *Language, literacy and power in schooling.* Mahwah, NJ: Lawrence Erlbaum Associates.

McDermott, R. (1977a). The ethnography of teaching and reading (pp. 153–185). In R.W. Shuy (Ed.), *Linguistic theory: What it can say about reading.* Newark, DE: International Reading Association.

McDermott, R. (1977b). School relations as contexts for learning in school. *Harvard Education Review*, 87, 299–313.

McDermott, R. & K. Gospodinoff (1991). Social contexts for ethnic borders and school failure (pp. 212–232). In H.T. Trueba, G.P Guthrie, and K.H. Au (Eds.), *Culture and the bilingual classroom*. Rowley, MA: Newbury House Publishers.

McDonald, M., E. Kazemi & S. Schneider Kavanagh (2013). A call for a common language and collective activity. *Journal of Teacher Education*, 20(10), 1–9.

McIntyre, E., A. Rosebery & N. Gonzalez (2001). *Classroom diversity: Connecting curriculum to students' lives*. Portsmouth, NH: Heinemann.

Mehan, H. (1979). *Learning lessons: Social organization in the classroom*. Cambridge MA: Harvard University Press.

Mehan, H. (1981). Ethnography for bilingual education. In H.T. Trueba, G.P. Guthrie, and K.H. Au (Eds.), *Culture and the bilingual classroom*. Rowley, MA: Newbury House Publishers.

Mercado, C.I. (2001). The learner: Race, ethnicity, and linguistic difference (A review of the literature) (pp. 668–691). In V. Richardson (Ed.), *Handbook of research on teaching*, 4th edn. Washington, DC: The American Educational Research Association.

Mercado, C.I. & C. Brochin-Ceballos (2011). Growing quality teachers: Community-oriented preparation. In B.B. Flores, R.H. Sheets, and E.R. Clark (Eds.), *Teacher preparation for bilingual student populations: Educar para transformar*. New York, NY: Taylor and Francis/Routledge.

Mercado, C. I. & L.C. Moll (1997). The study of funds of knowledge: Collaborative research in Latino homes. *CENTRO, Journal of the Center for Puerto Rican Studies*, 9(1), 27–42.

Mercado, C.I. & D. Oest (1992). Through the eyes of the teacher and the student: Reflective practice and reciprocal teaching in a bilingual graduate reading course. Paper presented at the annual meeting of the National Association of Education Albuquerque, NM, January, 1992.

Mercado, C.I. & M. Romero (1993). Assessment of students in bilingual education. In M. Beatriz Arias and U. Casanova (Eds.), *Bilingual education: Politics, practice, and research: Ninety-second yearbook of the National Society for the Study of Education*. Chicago, IL: NSSE.

Milem, J.F. (2003). The educational benefits of diversity: Evidence from multiple sectors (chapter 5). In M. Chang, D. Witt, and K. Hakuta (Eds.), *Compelling Interests: Examining the evidence on racial dynamics in higher education*. Palo Alto, CA: Stanford University Press.

Milner, H.R. (2013). Analyzing poverty, learning and teaching through a critical, race theory lens. *Review of Research in Education*, 37, 1–53.

Moll, L.C. (1988). Some key issues in teaching Latino students. *Language Arts*, 65(15), 465–471.

Moll, L.C. & E. Diaz (1980). An ethnography of bilingual classrooms. Final report. Washington, DC: National Institute of Education.

Moll, L.C. & E. Diaz (1987). Change as the goal of educational research. *Anthropology and Education Quarterly*, 18, 300–311.

Moll, L.C., C. Amanti, D. Neff & N. González (1992). Funds of knowledge for teaching: Using a qualitative approach to connect homes and classrooms. *Theory into Practice*, 23(2), 132–141.

Moll, L.C., E. Estrada, E. Diaz & L.M. Lopes (1980). The organization of bilingual lessons: Implications for schooling. *The Quarterly Newsletter of the Laboratory of Comparative Human Cognition*, 2(3), 53–58.

Murnane, R.J. & F. Levy (1996). *Teaching the new basic skills: Principles for educating children to thrive in a changing economy*. New York: The Free Press.

Muspratt, S., A. Luke & P. Freebody (Eds.) (1997). *Constructing critical literacies: Teaching and learning textual practice*. Cresskill, NJ: Hampton Press.

Nathenson-Mejias, S. & K. Escamilla (Spring, 2003). Connecting with Latino children's literature: Bridging cultural gaps and children's literature. *Bilingual Research Journal*, 27(1): 101–116.

National Reading Panel (1997). Teaching children to read: An evidence-based assessment of the scientific research literature on reading and its implications for reading instruction. NICHD. Available online: https://www.nichd.nih.gov/publications/pubs/nrp/smallbook

Neuman, S.B. (2001). The role of knowledge in early literacy. *Reading Research Quarterly*, 36(4), 468–475.

Nieto, S. (1983). Children's literature on Puerto Rican themes. *Bulletin of the Council on Interracial Books for Children*, 14(1/2), 10–16.

Nieto, S. (1993). We have stories to tell: A case study of Puerto Ricans in children's books. *Rethinking Schools*, 8(2), 20–23.

Ochs, E. (1988). *Culture and language development*. New York: Cambridge University Press.

Othaniel Smith, B. (1969). *Teachers for the real world*. Washington, DC: Association for Supervision and Curriculum Development.

Ovando, C.J. (2004). Teaching for social justice: A critique of No Child Left Behind. Paper presented at the California Association of Freirean Educators, February 28, 2004. Los Angeles, CA: Paulo Freire Institute, University of California at Los Angeles.

Panofsky, C.P. (2003). The relations of learning and student social class: Toward RE-"socializing" sociocultural learning theory (pp. 411–432). In K. Kozulin, B. Gindis, V.S. Ageyev, and S. Miller (Eds.), *Vygotsky's educational theory in cultural context*. Boston, MA: Cambridge University Press.

Paris, S.G. (December, 2003). What K-3 teachers need to know about assessing children's reading. Learning Point Associates (NCREL) (16 pp.).

Paris, D. (2012). Culturally sustaining pedagogy: A needed change in stance, terminology, and practice. *Educational Researcher*, 41, 93–97.

Paulston, C.P. (December, 1974). Linguistic and communicative competence. *TESOL Quarterly*, 8(4), 347–362.

Pea, R. (2009). Fostering learning in the networked world: Trends, opportunities and challenges for learning environments and education. 3rd Redesigning Pedagogy International Conference, National Institute of Education, Singapore. June 2, 2009.

Pedraza, P. (1987). *An ethnographic analysis of language use in the Puerto Rican community of East Harlem.* New York: Center for Puerto Rican Studies, Hunter College of CUNY.

Perez, B. (Ed.) (1998). *Sociocultural contexts of language and literacy.* Mahwah, NJ: Lawrence Erlbaum Associates.

Perrone, V. (1998). *Teacher with heart.* New York: Teachers College Press.

Pianta, R.C. & K. La Paro (2003). Improving early school success. *Education Leadership,* 60(7), 24–29.

Pianta, R.C., S. Rimm-Kaufman & M.J. Cox (1999). An ecological approach to kindergarten transition (chapter 2). In R.C. Pianta and M.J. Cox (Eds.), *The transition to kindergarten.* Baltimore, MD: Brookes Publishing.

Pickering, N. (2006). Learning about university teaching: Reflections on a research study investigating influences for change. *Teaching in Higher Education,* 11(3), 319–335.

Pinnegar, S. & M.I. Hamilton (2009). *The self, the other, and practice in self-study of teaching and teacher education practices research.* New York, NY: Springer International.

Portes, A. & R.G. Rumbaut (2001). The forging of a new America: lessons from theory and policy (pp. 301–317). In R.G. Rumbaut and A. Portes (Eds.), *Ethnicities— Children of immigrants in America.* Berkeley, CA: University of California Press.

Reyes, M.L. (1991). A process approach to literacy using dialogue journals and literature logs with second language learners. *Research in the Teaching of English,* 25(3), 291–313.

Reyes, M.L. (1997). Chicanas in academe: An endangered species (chapter 1). In S. de Castell and M. Bryson (Eds.), *Radical interventions.* Albany, NY: SUNY Press.

Reyes, L.O. (Chair) (1999). Making the vision a reality: A Latino action agenda for educational reform. Final report of the Latino Commission on Educational Reform, March 23, 1999.

Rigg, P. & V.G. Allen (1988). *When they don't all speak English: Integrating the ESL student into the regular classroom.* Urbana, IL: NCTE.

Rockwell, E. (2001). Reading as a cultural practice. *Educao Pesquisa, Sao Paulo,* 27(1), 11–26.

Rockwell, E. (2005). Indigenous accounts of dealing with writing (pp. 5–28). In T.L. McCarty (Ed.), *Language, literacy and power in schooling.* Mahwah NJ: Lawrence Erlbaum Associates, Publishers.

Rogoff, B. (1994). Developing understanding of the idea of community of learners. *Mind, Culture and Society,* 1(4), 209–229.

Romero, S. (2017). Spanish thrives in the US despite an English-only drive. *New York Times,* August 23, 2017.

Rosenblatt, L. (1988). Writing and reading: The transactional theory. Technical Report No. 13. National Center for the Study of Writing University of California at Berkeley, CA and Carnegie-Mellon University, Pittsburg, PA.

Roth, W-M. (2007). Emotion at work: A contribution to third-generation cultural-historical activity theory. *Mind, Culture, and Activity*, 14(1/2), 40–63.

Roth, W.M. & Y.T. Lee (2007). Vygotsky's neglected legacy: Cultural historical activity theory. *Review of Educational Research*, 77(2), 186–232.

Russell, T. & J. Loughran (1997). *Teaching about teaching: Purpose, passion and pedagogy in teacher education*. Bristol, PA: Falmer Press.

Russell, T. & J. Loughran (2007). *Enacting a pedagogy of teacher education: Values, relationships and practices*. New York: Routledge.

Russell, T. & F. Korthagen (1995). *Teachers who teach teachers. Reflections on teacher education*. London: Routledge Falmer.

Russo, A. (2012). Left out of No Child Left Behind. Teach for America's outsize influence on alternative certification. American Enterprise Institute for Public Policy Research.

Sahlberg, P. (2015). *Finnish lessons*. New York, NY: Teachers College Press.

Sánchez Korrol, V. (1983). *From colonia to community: The history of Puerto Ricans in New York City*. Westport, CT: Greenwood Press.

Sannino, A. (2011). Activity theory as an activist and interventionist theory. *Theory & Psychology*, 21(5), 571–597.

Santiago, R. (1995). *Boricuas: Influential Puerto Rican writing*. New York, NY: Random House Publishing Group.

Saul, W. & D. Dieckman (2005). Choosing and using information trade books. *Reading Research Quarterly*, 40(4), 502–513.

Shulman, L.S. (Spring, 2005). Pedagogies of uncertainty. *Liberal Education*, 18–25.

Shultz, K. & S.M. Ravitch (2013). Narratives of learning to teach. *Journal of Teacher Education*, 64(1), 35–46.

Sipe, L.R. (2000). The construction of literary understanding by first and second graders in oral response to picture storybook read-aloud. *Reading Research Quarterly*, 35(2), 252–275.

Sleeter, C.E. (2001). Epistemological diversity in research on pre-service teacher preparation for historically underserved children. *Review of Research in Education*, 25, 209–250.

Sloan, G. (2003) *The child as critic: Developing literacy through literature k-8*, 4th edn. New York, NY: Teachers College Press.

Smagorinsky, P. (1995). The social construction of data: Methodological problems of investigating learning in the zone of proximal development. *Review of Educational Research*, 65(3), 191–212.

Smagorinsky, P. (2017). Misfits in school literacy: Whom are U.S. schools designed to serve? (pp. 199–214). In D. Appleman and K. Hinchman (Eds.), *Adolescent literacy: A handbook of practice-based research*. New York, NY: Guilford.

Smagorinsky, P. (2018). Literacy in teacher education: It's the context, stupid. *Journal of Literacy Research*, 50(3), 281–303.

Smagorinsky, P. & M.E. Barnes (2014). Revisiting and revising the Apprenticeship of Observation. *Teacher Education Quarterly*, 41(4), 29–52.

Smith, F. (1978). *Reading*. Cambridge: Cambridge University Press.

Smyth, J. (1989). Developing and maintaining critical reflection in teacher education. *The Journal of Teacher Education*, 40(2), 94–103.

Snow, C.E., M.S. Burns & P. Griffin (Eds.) (1998). *Preventing reading difficulties in young children: National Research Council*. Washington DC: National Academy Press

Soja, E.W. (1996). *Third space: Journeys to Los Angeles and other real and imagined places*. Maiden, MA: Blackwell Publishers.

Stark, P.B. & R. Freishtat (June, 2014). An evaluation of course evaluations. Center for Teaching and Learning, University of California at Berkeley. Berkeley, CA.

Strauss, V. (2018). "A Nation at Risk" demanded education reform 35 years ago: Here's how it's been bungled every time. *The Washington Post*, April 29, 2018.

Street, B.V. (1995). *Social literacies: Critical approaches to literacy development, ethnography and education*. New York, NY: Longman Publishing.

Stromquist, N.P. & K. Monkman (Eds.) (2014). *Globalization and education: Integration and contestation across cultures*, 2nd edn. Lanham, MD: Roman & Littlefield Publishers.

Sulzby, E. (1985). Children's emergent reading of favorite storybook: A developmental study. *Reading Research Quarterly*, 20(4), 244–279.

Sumara, D. (2002). *Why reading literature in school still matters*. Mahwah NJ: Lawrence Erlbaum Associates.

Tatto, M.T. (2011). Reimagining the education of teachers: The role of comparative and international research. *Comparative Education Review*, 55(4), 495–516.

Taylor, D. & C. Dorsey-Gaines (1988). *Growing up literate*. Portsmouth, NH: Heinemann.

Teale, W.H. (1984). Reading to young children: Its significance for literacy development. In H. Goelman, A. Oberg, and F. Smith (Eds.), *Awakening to literacy*. Exeter, NH: Heinemann.

Teale, W.H. & E. Sulzby (1986). *Emergent literacy as a perspective in examining how young children become readers and writers*. Westport, CT: Praeger.

Tharp, R. & R. Gallimore (1988). *Rousing minds to life: Teaching, learning, schooling in social contexts*. Cambridge, MA: Cambridge University Press.

Thonis, E. (1991). Competencies for teachers of language minority students. In M. McGroarty and C. Faltis (Eds.), *Languages in school and society: Policy and pedagogy*. Berlin: Mouton de Gruyter.

The National Commission on Excellence in Education (April, 1983). A nation at risk: The imperative for educational reform. Washington, DC: US Department of Education.

Tikunoff, W. (1985). *Applying bilingual instructional features in the classroom.* Rosslyn, VA: National Clearinghouse for Bilingual Education.

Torres, C.A. (2009). *Education and neoliberal globalization.* New York, NY: Routledge.

Travieso, L. (1975). Puerto Ricans and education. *Journal of Teacher Education*, 26(2), 128–30.

Trinidad Galvan, R. (2010). Calming the spirit and insuring supervivencia: Rural Mexican women-centered teaching and learning spaces. *Ethnography and Education*, 5(3), 309–323.

Trueba, H.T., G.P. Guthrie & K.H. Au (1981). *Culture and the bilingual classroom.* Rowley, MA: Newbury House Publishers.

Urciuoli, B. (1996). *Exposing prejudice: Puerto Rican experiences of language, race, and class.* Boulder, CO: Westview Press.

Urciuoli, B. (1999). The political topography of Spanish and English: The view from a New York Puerto Rican neighborhood. *American Ethnologist*, 18(2), 295–310.

Valdes, G. (1991). Bilingual minorities and language issues in writing: Toward profession-wide responses to a new challenge. Technical report no. 54. University of Berkeley, Berkeley, CA: Center for the Study of Writing.

Valdes-Fallis, G. (1978). A comprehensive approach to the teaching of Spanish to bilingual Spanish-speaking students. *The Modern Language Journal*, 62(3), 102–110.

Van Manen, M. (1990). *Researching lived experience.* New York, NY: State University of New York Press.

Vygotsky, L.S. ([1934] 1987). Thinking and speech (pp. 39–285). In *The collected works of L.S. Vygotsky. Volume 1.* R.W. Rieber and A. Carton (Eds.), N. Minick (trans.), New York, NY: Plenum.

Vygotsky, L.S. (1993). *The collected works of L.S. Vygotsky. Volume 2: The fundamentals of defectology (abnormal psychology and learning disabilities).* R.W. Rieber & A.S. Carton (Eds.), J.E. Knox & C.B. Stevens, (trans.). New York, NY: Plenum.

Weiner, B. (2007). Examining emotional diversity in the classroom: An attribution theorist considers the moral emotions (pp. 75–88). In P.A. Schutz and R. Pekrun (Eds.), Educational psychology series. *Emotion in education.* San Diego, CA: Elsevier.

Weis, L. (1999). *Urban teaching.* New York, NY: Teachers College Press.

Weisner, T.S. (2002). Ecocultural understanding of children's developmental pathways. *Human Development*, 45, 275–281.

Wells, G. (1990). Creating the conditions for literate thinking. *Educational Leadership*, 47(6), 13–17.

Wells, G. (1995). Language and the inquiry-oriented curriculum. *Curriculum Inquiry*, 25(3), 233–269.

Wells, G. & G.J. Chang (1990). *Constructing knowledge together: Classrooms as centers of inquiry and learning.* Portsmouth, NH: Heinemann.

Wideen, M., J. Mayer-Smith & B. Moon (Summer, 1998). A critical analysis of the research on learning to teach. *Review of Educational Research*, 68(2), 130–178.

Wilson, E.O. (Spring, 2002). The power of story. *American Federation of Teachers* (8–12).

Winograd, P. & S.G. Paris (1988). A cognitive and motivational agenda for reading instruction. *Educational Leadership*, 46(4), 30–36.

Wolf, S.A. (2004). *Interpreting literature with children*. Mahwah, NJ: Lawrence Erlbaum Associates.

Wong-Fillmore, L. (1982). Instructional language as linguistic input: Second language learning in classroom (pp. 283–296). In L.C. Wilkinson (Ed.), *Communicating in the classroom*. New York: Academic Press.

Wong-Fillmore, L. (1991). Language and cultural issues in the early education of language minority children (pp. 30–49). In S. Kagan (Ed.), *The care and education of America's young children: Obstacles and opportunities. Ninetieth Yearbook of the National Society for the Study of Education Part I*. Chicago, IL: University of Chicago Press.

Wong-Fillmore, L. (2000). What teachers need to know about language. Clearinghouse on Languages and Linguistics. Special Report, August 23, 2000.

Wong-Fillmore, L. (2010). Common Core Standards: Can English learners meet them? (Online PowerPoint presentation, September 27–28, 2010).

Wong-Fillmore, L. & C.J. Fillmore (n.d.). Understanding language. Language, literacy and learning in the content areas. What does text complexity mean for English learners and language minority students? Stanford University School of Education.

Woodard, V. (1985). Collaborative pedagogy: Researcher and teacher learning together. *Langauge Arts*, 62(7), 770–776.

Young, I. (2005). Responsibility and social justice: A social connection model. Prepared for a presentation on global justice at Bowling Green State University, Bowling Green, Ohio, October 21–23, 2004.

Zaidi, A.S. (2010). Essentialist stereotypes in textbooks on Hispanic studies (pp. 227–238). In M. Telmissany and S.T. Schwartz (Eds.), *Counterpoints: Edward Said's legacy*. Newcastle: Cambridge Scholars Publishing.

Zeichner, K., K.A. Payne & K. Brayko (2015). Democratizing teacher education. *Journal of Teacher Education*, 66(2), 122–135.

Zentella, A.C. (1997). *Growing up bilingual: Puerto Rican children in New York*. Oxford: Blackwell Press.

Zentella, A.C. (Ed.) (2005). *Building on strengths: Language and literacy in Latino families and communities*. New York, NY: Teachers College Press.

Index

Note: Page numbers in *italics* indicate figures.

Lightning Source UK Ltd.
Milton Keynes UK
UKHW032313301020
372527UK00005B/282